THE SECOND CENTURY FUND · ABBOT PUBLIC LIBRARY · MARBLEHEAD ·

Donated By

THE SECOND CENTURY FUND

Preserving A Tradition Of
Citizen Philanthropy

Robert Browning Revisited

Twayne's English Authors Series

Herbert Sussman, Editor

Northeastern University

TEAS 530

PORTRAIT OF ROBERT BROWNING BY GEORGE FREDERIC WATTS.
By courtesy of the National Portrait Gallery, London.

Robert Browning Revisited

Adam Roberts

Royal Holloway, University of London

Twayne Publishers
An Imprint of Simon & Schuster Macmillan
New York

Prentice Hall International
London • Mexico City • New Delhi • Singapore • Sydney • Toronto

Twayne's English Authors Series No. 530

Robert Browning Revisited
Adam Roberts

Copyright 1996 by Twayne Publishers

Twayne Publishers
An Imprint of Simon & Schuster Macmillan
1633 Broadway
New York, New York 10019

Library of Congress Cataloging-in-Publication Data

Roberts, Adam (Adam Charles)
  Robert Browning revisited / Adam Roberts.
     p.   cm. — (Twayne's English authors series ; no. 530)
  Includes bibliographical references and index.
  ISBN 0-8057-4590-4 (alk. paper)
    1. Browning, Robert, 1812–1889—Criticism and interpretation.
I. Title. II. Series: Twayne's English authors series ; TEAS 530.
PR4238.R596   1996
821'.8—dc20
                      96-33243
                      CIP

Contents

Preface

Despite its fluctuations this century, Browning's reputation is now high. This is partly because his poetry manages the surprising trick of providing satisfying and challenging reading for two apparently disparate groups of modern readers, the traditionalists and the radical theoreticians. There are enough of the good old-fashioned literary virtues to keep the former group happy—a subtle and effective sense of form and structure, a profound humanism, an expert sense of character and narrative, and a rigorous ethical grounding. But at the same time, Browning's experiments with form and his challenging and disruptive style—indeed, arguably his entire aesthetic—embody the most radical concerns of those interested in radical literary theory. It hardly overstates the case to regard Browning as a sort of deconstructionist *avant la lettre*, although (as I argue in this study) the parallel is not exact.

This study has been undertaken with a variety of aims in view. One prompt has been a desire to cater to the needs of both the aforementioned groups of readers. I have tried not to make my work theoretically or methodologically doctrinaire, although I have found many modern theoretical readings of Browning very useful, and that fact is reflected in what follows. I try to enter into the contemporary debates about Browning without particularly siding with one position or another in order not to compromise a more basic aim. The primary purpose of this study is to provide an accessible introduction and overview of Browning's poetic career. To this end the chapters are arranged chronologically; thematic issues (Browning's style, Browning and women, and so forth) are introduced where they seem most appropriate, and the events of Browning's life are related to his work where such a reading seems relevant.

The thesis of the book, such as it has one, sees Browning the poet as the product of a dialectical engagement between Romantic subjectivity and Victorian objectivity. The urge to look inward, to detail the life of the mind, that we might identify with the shorthand term *Romantic*, was tempered in Browning with the need to look outward, to ground his poetics in some sense of objective reality, a more typically Victorian concern. In the latter portion of the study, in particular, I explore the ways this shaping dialectic informs the mature Browning with a deep-rooted binarism, a tendency to articulate poetic vision via oppositional pairs. Of special importance is the aesthetic that the mature Browning elaborates, which is one of spontaneity and energy as opposed to aridity and legalism.

Another central contention of this study is that the neglect of the later Browning (which is to say, the material published after *The Ring and the Book*), of which virtually all critical studies of Browning are guilty, is not only unjustified but fatally distorting. The merits of the post–*Ring and the Book* writings are so plain, it seems to me, that there is no need to further justify the lengthy attention I pay to this part of Browning's career. Only with a complete sense of Browning's whole career can a student fully come to terms with the enormity of his contribution to modern literature.

Any critic who seeks to deal with an author as voluminous and sophisticated as Browning in so short a space, with one eye always on the imperative implied in the tag *introductory*, is going to find the constraints almost insurmountable. I have not been able to deal with every poem written by Browning, although I have tried to include all significant publications. Where possible, I have also tried to provide original readings of Browning's output. Due to the huge amount of critical work done on Browning's early period, the importance of traditional critical debates, and the need to put a great deal of basic information into a short space, my original readings are mostly confined to the second half of the study. But there, from chapter six (*Dramatis Personae*) onward, the proportion of entirely new criticism is high.

I quote Browning's poetry from John Pettigrew and Thomas Collins, eds., *Robert Browning: The Poems*, 2 vols. (Harmondsworth, England: Penguin, 1981) and Richard Altick, ed., *The Ring and the Book* (Harmondsworth, England: Penguin, 1971).

Chronology

1812   Born on May 7 at Camberwell, London, to Robert and Sara Anna Wiedemann Browning.

1824   Browning's parents try without success to publish his first collection of poems, *Incondita*. The manuscript is later destroyed.

1826   First reads Shelley's *Miscellaneous Poems* and *Queen Mab*. Falls under Shelley's influence, and declares himself an atheist and a vegetarian.

1828   Enters London University, but does not last the year.

1833   *Pauline* published anonymously. It sinks virtually without trace.

1834   Travels to Russia. Applies unsuccessfully for a diplomatic post.

1835   *Paracelsus* published at his father's expense. Some modest fame results.

1837   *Strafford* performed at Covent Garden. It is not successful.

1838   First journey to Italy.

1840   *Sordello* published. It immediately forges a reputation for impenetrable obscurity and literary affectation.

1841   Begins publishing a series of poetic pamphlets, *Bells and Pomegranates*, aimed at reaching a popular audience (the title alludes to a rabbinical coupling of "pleasure and profit"). The first comprises *Pippa Passes*.

1842   *Bells and Pomegranates II: King Victor and King Charles* and *III:Dramatic Lyrics*.

1843   *Bells and Pomegranates IV: The Return of the Druses* and *V: A Blot in the 'Scutcheon*.

1844   Second journey to Italy. *Bells and Pomegranates VI: Colombe's Birthday*.

1845   *Bells and Pomegranates VII: Dramatic Romances and Lyrics*. Writes first letter to Elizabeth Barrett on January 10. The difficult and (in the face of her father's insistence that his daughter not marry) secret courtship begins with Browning's first visit on May 20.

1846   *Bells and Pomegranates VIII: Luria; A Soul's Tragedy.* Secretly marries Elizabeth Barrett on September 12. The couple leaves England for Italy on September 19.

1847   The couple settles in Florence, at a house called Casa Guidi.

1849   *Poems*, first collected edition. March 9 sees the birth of the couple's only child, Robert Weidemann Barrett Browning (known as "Pen").

1850   *Christmas-Eve and Easter Day.*

1852   The "Essay on Shelley."

1855   *Men and Women.* The couple visit London in the winter.

1857   A friend's legacy of £11,000 ensures financial security for the Brownings.

1860   Chances upon the *Old Yellow Book* at a stall in Florence.

1861   Death of Elizabeth Barrett Browning (June 29). Browning leaves Florence, never to return, and eventually settles in London.

1863   *The Poetical Works* (3 vols.).

1864   *Dramatis Personae.* Browning enjoys widespread critical and popular success for the first time. Begins work on *The Ring and the Book.*

1868   *The Poetical Works* (4 vols.).

1868–1869   *The Ring and the Book* published in four installments, from November to February. Very well received. Browning's popularity rivals Tennyson's.

1871   *Balaustion's Adventure; Prince Hohenstiel-Schwangau.*

1872   *Fifine at the Fair.*

1873   *Red Cotton Night-Cap Country.*

1874   *Aristophanes' Apology; The Inn Album.*

1876   *Pacchiarotto and How He Worked in Distemper.*

1877   Translates the *Agamemnon* of Aeschylus.

1878   *La Saisiaz* and *The Two Poets of Croisic.*

1879   *Dramatic Idyls, First Series.*

Chapter One
Beginning Browning: *Pauline*

I. Beginnings

Browning's life and Browning's art form a curious pairing. While there are inevitable linkages, places where biography informs the poetry, the overall relationship is one of dislocation. Henry James, who knew Browning in later life, was struck by the difference between the thoroughly ordinary figure of Browning the man on the one hand, and the extraordinary products of Browning the poet on the other. In his short story "The Private Life" (1892) he dramatized his uneasiness. In that tale, Browning is represented by the character of Claude Vaudrey, a profoundly original and brilliant novelist who is profoundly unoriginal and run-of-the-mill as a man. "I never found him anything but loud and cheerful and copious," says the story's narrator; "and I never ceased to ask myself, in this particular loud, sound, normal, hearty presence . . . all bristling with prompt response and expected opinions and usual views . . . what lodgement on such premises the rich proud genius one adored could ever have contrived." In the story the narrator eventually concludes that there are actually *two* identical Claude Vaudreys, never seen together, one writing the literature, one living the social life.

James's thumbnail sketch of Browning's character is a useful place to start; it functions almost as an apology in advance. To begin by detailing Browning's biographical circumstances is to risk obscuring the fact of his daring and extreme genius under the humdrum quietude of the facts of his life. Browning's poetry has often been spoken of in terms of violence. It marks a revolution in English poetics: its syntax appears mangled and distorted; its subjects are frequently violent madmen, murderers, and self-mutilators. But Browning's own background and life were so uneventful and tranquil as to stand in complete contrast.

Robert Browning was born on May 7, 1812, in the then pleasant village of Camberwell, just outside London. Here he spent a happy and untroubled youth, growing up in the company of mother and father and one sister, Sarianna. Robert Browning Senior was a mild-mannered man with a passion for reading; his library contained some six thousand books, many rare and valuable and all carefully annotated. This resource helped shape Robert's youth; it was from his father that Browning acquired a passionate love for literature, a love that sometimes lends his poetry a somewhat intimidating erudition but that also contributes to a dense and subtle texture of allusion and intertextuality. From his mother, Browning derived a deeply held and liberal Christianity. He remained close to both parents until their deaths.

The familial environment that shaped Browning was loving and secure. His father worked as a clerk at the Bank of England (a post he held until 1852), but both parents came from well-to-do middle-class stock, and Robert and his sister (who were close) were privately educated and encouraged to follow their impulses. "By the indulgence of my father and mother," Browning recalled later,

> I was allowed to live my own life and choose my own course in it; which, having been the same from the beginning to the end, necessitated a permission to read nearly all sorts of books, in a well-stocked and very miscellaneous library. I had no other direction but my parents' taste for whatever was highest and best in literature; but I found out for myself many forgotten fields which proved the richest of pastures.[1]

Browning enrolled at the newly formed University of London in October, 1828, for classes in Latin, Greek, and German; but he found that student life did not agree with him and withdrew May 1829. He considered (prompted by his father) a career as a doctor, but decided against it after a visit to Guy's Hospital. In 1834 he spent three months traveling in Russia as an aide to the Russian consul general in London, and he may have contemplated a diplomatic career himself; but the journey had more to do with expanding his mind through experience and thereby improving his poetry. Thereafter, Browning made no career moves at all; he was quite content to live at home, read, and write poetry. Indeed, from a biographical perspective, there is very little to say about so uneventful a growing-up.

The real interest in this period is located not in external events, but in Browning's intellectual and aesthetic development. While his outward circumstances were placid and settled, the young Browning underwent a series of turbulent and fiercely debated internal changes. Browning had written poetry since his earliest years; a collection of poetry assembled in his 12th year (modestly entitled *Incondita*, "unknown") had so impressed his parents that they had shown it to friends in hopes of finding a publisher. Only two of these early poems remain ("The Dance of Death" and "Fire, Famine, and Slaughter"), which makes the overall quality of *Incondita* difficult to judge; but it is clear that Browning himself thought the volume weak and imitative, and nobody could be found to publish it. He destroyed the manuscript and considered music (a lifelong passion) as an alternative means of expressing himself. A turning point came late in 1826, when Browning's cousin James Silverthorne presented him with a pirated edition of Shelley's *Miscellaneous Poems*—pirated because, in the 1820s, Shelley was still considered a dangerous political radical and atheist, and publishers had been prosecuted for printing him. A little later Browning managed to obtain Shelley's *Queen Mab*.

II. Browning and Romanticism: Shelley

When it comes to discussing the influences that shaped the young Browning, there is really no way around Percy Bysshe Shelley. Not just poetically, but ethically and politically—we might say, ideologically— Shelley was the pole star by which the young Browning oriented himself. Although Browning in later life felt himself estranged from his former hero (an estrangement that came about largely because of his belated discovery of Shelley's abandonment of his first wife), Shelley's impact on him was too deep to be erased by middle-aged indignation. The young Browning pored devotedly over his volumes of Shelley, studying the verse and absorbing everything it represented. Indeed, what Browning undertook was the assimilation, and supersession, of the most radical of the poets of Romanticism. In tracing the path from Shelley to Browning, we can see the shift from Romantic to Victorian poetry.

Of course, all such pigeonholing of literary "periods" is bound to tend toward the arbitrary; yet the transition from Romanticism to Victorianism is among the most pronounced in literary history. The second generation of Romantic poets all died in the 1820s (Keats in 1820, Shelley in 1822, and Byron in 1824); Coleridge and Wordsworth both lived longer, but neither wrote anything of great importance after the 1820s. Influenced by these writers as they inevitably were, poets publishing in the 1830s (Tennyson's first volume of poetry appeared in 1830, Browning's in 1833) were working in a markedly *post*-Romantic situation. The challenge was to wrestle with powerful Romantic influences and yet create a poetry that was not merely imitative, to write something distinctive and original. And while Browning knew and loved Byron (the remaining verses from *Incondita* display Byronic touches) and Wordsworth (evident in the lyric "The Lost Leader"), it was Shelley who was his prime inspiration, the shaping force. It is not too much to say that, for a number of years, (in the words of one of Browning's friends) "Shelley was his God."[2] He announced himself to be, after Shelley's example, not merely a vegetarian (which was bad enough in conventional, middle-class Camberwell), but an atheist—something calculated to be profoundly shocking to his pious mother.

The effect of Shelley on Browning's intellectual development was of the most radical kind. It is not a question of superficial rebellion (the vegetarianism and atheism lasted only a short while) but of an ongoing reassessment of all his basic beliefs. In a sense, this constituted an act of rebellion against the middle-class certainty into which he had been born, but for Browning there was actually very little to rebel against. Neither of his parents was authoritarian—quite the reverse in fact. Robert Browning Senior was a mild-mannered and liberal man, whose opposition to the slave trade (something he had encountered in his own youth) won him "infinite glory" in his son's eyes. Sarah Browning's Christianity, despite its Scottish Protestant roots, was nevertheless of a benign and loving kind. But Shelley encouraged Browning to question everything; and if no great changes resulted, that fact was less important than the process of questioning undergone—the interpreting of the world with an active intelligence.

The relationship between Browning and Romanticism is complex, but its most important aspect might be summed up by the word *psychological*. Romantic writers were revolutionary in their reassessment of the human mind, in the ways in which consciousness interacts with reality. Wordworth's masterwork *The Prelude* is subtitled "The Growth of a Poet's Mind"; in a sense, all of Browning's poetry interrogates precisely that theme. It is something particularly clear in the earlier work. *Pauline*, *Paracelsus*, and *Sordello* are centrally concerned with the development of mind or "Soul" (to use Browning's term). These poems tell us little about the external events of the protagonist's life, not because these events are irrelevant, but because in Browning's aesthetic they are necessarily subordinate to the inner life of the protagonist's mind. For this reason Browning's narrative line, judged in terms of traditional plot, is often difficult to follow, elaborated obliquely, if at all. This was a major reason for the label of "obscurity" that contemporary critics attached to Browning's name. In fact, even his most obscure works become considerably easier to understand when read in these terms.

At the core of Romanticism's fascination with questions of identity and psychology was its obsession with the process of the imagination (often written with a capital *I*) and the shaping power of the mind. This focus manifested itself in a great number of poems about poetry, or, to be more precise, poems about poets and the ways they produce poetry. Wordsworth, as we have seen, wrote an epic and autobiographical "Growth of a Poet's Mind"; Coleridge produced a dense, autobiographical study of the imagination, the *Biographia Literaria*. Byron closely resembled his own creations Childe Harold and Don Juan. Browning himself began his writing career working and reworking the theme of the development of the poet: *Pauline* autobiographically explores the influences on a sensitive young poet; *Paracelsus* involves the Shelleyan poet Aprile; and the hero of Browning's first epic, *Sordello*, taken from history, is a 13th-century Provençal poet.

Poets writing poetry about poets writing poetry: there is something rather involuted, something solipsistic and unhealthy, about this situation. The first ten years of Browning's writing career see him coming to terms with the dangers of this perspective on the self. Self-interrogation can lead to self-obsession, and the poet who focuses too intently on him- or herself runs the risk, as it were, of vanishing into the realms of morbid introspection. That there is a genuine danger of following this Romantic self-orientation too far was demonstrated by one of the dominant poetic schools of the early Victorian period, the Spasmodics. Little read today, this school continued Romantic trends to the point of self-parody, and even in their own day poets such as Sidney Dobell and Alexander Smith excited considerable ridicule. They are interesting for the student of Browning insofar as they show the sort of career Browning might, on the evidence of his first three major works, have developed, but that, as we shall see, he managed to avoid.

Works such as Marston's *Gerald* (1842), Bailey's *Festus* (1839), Smith's *A Life Drama* (1853) and Dobell's *Balder* (1854) all concern the fortunes of struggling poets—and all are static works, the interest being the interior landscape of the protagonist, articulated in a stream of images and over-excited passages. The problems cited by critics of the Spasmodics (lack of structure, verbosity, a tendency toward the ludicrous) are actually secondary. The main problem is that the aesthetic behind the Spasmodics is so involuted it effectively throttles itself. Where the great Romantics balance their analysis of the mind with an awareness of the way the mind relates to the not-self, the Spasmodics are really concerned only with internal monologue. Dobell's *Balder* provides an example. Balder is a poet who lives in a tower with his wife, Amy. He is in the process of writing an epic poem. Much of Dobell's epic is taken up with its protagonist reading from his own epic; the rest of the time, Dobell is talking about himself and his view of the world. Eventually, after what seems a very long time, Amy goes mad; by this stage, the reader is liable to sympathize with her. When Balder tries to murder her, Dobell is actually dramatizing the text collapsing under its own weight. The Spasmodic self-consciousness was, literally, untenable: not able to support itself, it turned the Spasmodic experiment into a literary dead-end. If *Pauline*, *Paracelsus*, or *Sordello* sometimes have a Spasmodic feel, they are redeemed by Browning's struggle to escape from self-consciousness, to balance subjectivity with a form of objectivity.

The dangers of falling under the spell of the Romantics are clear enough. Shelley inspired Browning to become a great poet, and consequently Browning began by writing like Shelley. But, clearly, Browning needed to supersede Shelley, to move out from Shelley's shadow and find his own voice, in order to become a poet worth reading. In fact, Shelley himself provided Browning with the ammunition to escape: he was just as fascinated with the need to engage (and reform) the external world as with the internal workings of the poet's mind. Indeed, for Shelley, the point in concentrating on the internal is to be able to free one's mind from preconception and oppression and thereby be in a better position to engage in revolutionary political reform.

Shelley's central insight concerns the necessity of undertaking one's own interpretive endeavor. Shelley's *Alastor* (1816)—another poem about a poet—sounds a warning note: its hero wanders away from human company, thoroughly alienated, and goes into the wilderness to die. The moral on one level seems to be that too much introspection is bad for you. *Queen Mab* (1813), on the other hand, is a visionary philosophical and ideological work whose blank verse attacks on monarchy, commerce, and religion are augmented by lengthy prose footnotes. One does not need to agree with everything argued to understand the moral—that (to paraphrase Karl Marx's dictum) it is not enough to merely interpret the world, the point is to change it.

Although Browning was never as politically active as was Shelley (his few adolescent months of experimental atheism and vegetarianism aside), political engagement is a theme that runs through all of his work. He declared his political philosophy in the sonnet "Why I Am a Liberal" and was always ready to involve himself in certain causes (the antislavery movement, for instance) in which he believed. Many of his poems dissect the workings of the political mind (*Prince Hohenstiel-Schwangau* preeminently), and from the earliest Browning debated with himself the extent to which it is possible to involve oneself in political power without becoming corrupted by it (Sordello decides that it is better to avoid established politics altogether). But there is something more important here than a particular hue of political affiliation: Browning learned from Shelley that while the examination of the life of the mind is central to poetry, it is not sufficient unto itself. It needs to be tempered with a sense of the outside world if it is not to vanish into morbid self-consciousness.

Browning's most intense passion for Shelley did not really outlast his youth, but this is an influence evident throughout his career. A poem written in the 1850s, "Memorabilia," illustrates how long the impact of Shelley lasted. Browning recalled, "I was one day in the shop of Hodgson, the well-known London bookseller, when a stranger . . . spoke of something that Shelley had once said to him. Suddenly the stranger paused, and burst into laughter as he observed me staring at him with blanched face; and I still remember how strangely the presence of a man who had seen and spoken with Shelley affected me."[3]

I

Ah, did you once see Shelley plain,
    And did he stop and speak to you?
And did you speak to him again?
    How strange it seems and new!

II

But you were living before that,
    And also you are living after;
And the memory I started at—
    My starting moves your laughter.

This is a memory Browning "started" at in more senses than one. As we have seen, his poetic career literally started with the impact Shelley had on him; and the poem's title (which means "things worth remembering") suggests that Browning had not forgotten his poetic origins. The extreme nature of the reaction is appropriate for a man meeting his "god." In his later poetry Browning works through this theme in a more conventionally religious manner: poems such as "A Death in the Desert," "An Epistle . . . of Karshish" and "Cleon" are about the presence of Christ. Yet each is narrated not by somebody who actually met Christ but by somebody who has met somebody who knew Christ (in the case of "A Death in the Desert," by somebody who has met somebody who has met somebody who has met Christ). This belatedness, the deferral of authoritative presence, is very much to the point, as we shall see. Truth, that central concern of Browning's work, is never something we can apprehend immediately; we can only know it at secondhand. For Shelley, the distance is one that Browning was forced to increase in order to find himself poetic space to grow. "Memorabilia" concludes,

III

I crossed a moor, with a name of its own
   And a certain use in the world no doubt,
Yet a hand's-breadth of it shines alone
   'Mid the blank miles round about:

IV

For there I picked up on the heather
   And there I put inside my breast
A moulted feather, an eagle-feather!
   Well, I forget the rest.

The close is beautifully judged, that seemingly offhand final line so eloquently understating the impossibility of properly articulating the full importance of Shelley to the poet.

In "Memorabilia," Shelley is described in terms of an eagle. In *Pauline* he is referred to as the "Sun-Treader" and addressed in terms of pure hero-worship:

Sun-treader—life and light be thine for ever;
Thou art gone from us—years go by—and spring
Gladdens, and the young earth is beautiful,
Yet thy songs come not—other bards arise,
But none like thee . . .
The air seems bright with past presence yet. (151–161)

Shelley is also one of the key figures behind Aprile, the poet who
appears in Part II of *Paracelsus*. By the time of *Sordello*, Shelley is invoked
specifically in order to be banished from the enterprise:

> thou, spirit, come not near
> Now—nor this time desert thy cloudy place
> To scare me, thus employed, with that pure face! . . .
> . . . this is no place for thee! (1.60–64]

Sordello has no place for Shelley because Browning has chosen to write in
an epic mode, which contrasts with Shelley's primarily lyric manner. But
it is interesting that Browning should talk of being "scared" by the
approach of Shelley. It is as if Browning is struggling with a too-power-
ful grip. If *Sordello* sees Browning breaking away from the influence of
high Romanticism and Shelley, then it is part of a process that took over
a decade, the same process by which Browning found his own poetic
voice.

III. The "Essay on Shelley"

Shelley is also useful for our purposes here because he forms the subject
of Browning's only significant piece of critical prose. In 1851 a friend of
Browning's, the publisher Edward Moxon, approached him to write an
introduction to an edition of *The Letters of Percy Bysshe Shelley*. Browning
welcomed the chance to try and put down in words exactly why Shelley
had meant so much to him over the years, and in doing so, he made a
rare attempt to articulate his own theory of poetry.

One reason why this piece of work (sometimes called the "Essay on
Shelley" and sometimes the "Introductory Essay"[4]) is deemed so valuable by Browning critics is its virtual uniqueness. Browning almost
never put his thoughts about poetry (especially his own poetry) into critical prose; explication of this kind was anathema to him. Where many
poets leave behind them large bodies of critical writings in prose,
Browning left virtually nothing.

I cite the "Essay on Shelley" here, despite the fact that it is the product of a later period in Browning's life, because the two types of poet it
discusses—"Subjective" and "Objective"—are crucial concepts if we
want to comprehend the way Browning's own poetic career developed.
It helps define Browning's understanding of the difference between a

Romantic poet such as Shelley and a Victorian poet such as himself. To
define these two categories he draws on the rhetoric of German thought
of the 1820s, as mediated by Coleridge's later prose. On the one hand
there is the "objective poet":

> one whose endeavour has been to reproduce things external (whether the
> phenomena of the scenic universe, or the manifested action of the human
> heart and brain) with an immediate reference, in every case, to the com-
> mon eye and appearance of his fellow men.

Browning's example of an "objective" poet is Shakespeare, a man who
"created" a tremendous wealth of differentiated, external characters, but
about whom we know next to nothing.

On the other hand, according to Browning, there is the "subjective
poet":

> He, gifted like the objective poet with the fuller perception of nature and
> man, is impelled to embody the thing he perceives, not so much with ref-
> erence to the many below as to the One above him, the supreme Intelli-
> gence which apprehends all things in their absolute truth. . . . He does
> not paint pictures and hang them on the walls, but rather carries them
> on the retina of his own eyes.

Such a poet is a "seer" whose work is an "effluence" from his own personality; Browning considered Shelley to be the supreme example of this
sort of poet. Browning highly valued "subjective" poetry: as far as he
was concerned, it was the more unified and truthful form of art. His
own poetic skills (he came to believe) were too fragmented. In a letter to
Elizabeth Barrett, written before they were married, he praises her
poetry over his own in these terms:

> You *do* what I always wanted, hoped to do—you speak out, *you*,—I only
> make men & women speak—give you the truth broken into prismatic
> hues, and fear the pure white light. (January 13, 1845)

Of course, the conception of poetry as "the very radiance and aroma of
[the poet's] personality, projected from it but not separated" ("Essay on
Shelley") is intensely Romantic; and Victorianism tended to define itself
in opposition to this "subjective" version of the poetic. Matthew Arnold's
very influential "Preface to *Poems*" (1853), for instance, suggests that
something had gone wrong with poetry during the period of the Roman-

tics and that modern poets should return to the ancient Greeks as models and inspirations. The Greeks had "calm," "cheerfulness," and "objectivity"; but in Romantic poetry, "the dialogue of the mind with itself had commenced," and the result was poetry that was "painful" to the reader. Arnold prioritizes "disinterested objectivity" as the prime poetic aim. Browning's views were less one-sided. He was drawn to the "subjective" form of poetry, with its inward-gazing search for ultimate truth; but his own skills, he recognized, were more "objective."

It is useful, if a little anachronistic, to think of these two terms (objective and subjective) as the twin poles of Browning's aesthetic during this early, experimental period. A subjective, Shelleyan vision inspired him to write poetry that was then informed by his attempt to develop an objective, Victorian voice. The tension between these two forces was something Browning could not fully reconcile for nearly fifteen years.

IV. *Pauline*

Browning's first published work grew out of a dramatic event. On October 22, 1832, Browning went to Richmond to see the great but worn-out Romantic actor Edmund Kean play Shakespeare's villainous Richard III. For some reason, the performance touched a chord in Browning. On the journey back home to Camberwell he hatched a plan for an elaborate artistic project: to create a series of works, each of a different sort (poem, novel, opera, and so on) and each apparently written by a different person. Browning himself explains in a preface he scribbled in one copy of the published work:

> The following Poem was written in pursuance of a foolish plan . . . which had for its object the enabling me to assume and realize I know not how many different characters;—meanwhile the world was never to guess that "Brown, Smith, Jones & Robinson" . . . the respective Authors of this poem, the other novel, such an opera, such a speech &c &c were no other than one and the same individual. The present abortion was the first work of the *Poet* of the batch.[5]

What is interesting here is that Browning sees himself as acting a series of roles—novelist, composer of operas, and so on. Indeed, it is worth stressing this aspect of the work in view of the common critical assessment of *Pauline* as an autobiographical, almost confessional poem. In fact, the dramatic (as opposed to subjective) aspect of the composition is predominant. The poem ends with a subscription, "RICHMOND, October 22, 1832," the place and date where Browning had seen Kean perform. Kean appears in the poem as well—the narrator imagines himself in Kean's situation (and possibly as Kean himself) as an aging and decaying actor gathering his energies for one last performance:

> I will be gifted with a wondrous soul,
> Yet sunk by error to men's sympathy,
> And in the wane of life; yet only so
> As to call up their fears, and there shall come
> A time requiring youth's best energies;
> And strait I fling age, sorrow, sickness off,
> And I rise triumphing over my decay. (669–675)[6]

There is perhaps something a little affected in a twenty-year-old man, writing at the commencement of his career, thinking himself into a character "in the wane of life." Yet the young poet was expressing at least as much legitimate ambition as affectation: he was trying to throw off the yoke of age from a whole artistic era, Romanticism. He was mustering his own youth and using it to inspire the old Romantic genius to new heights. The concept of "drama" is central to his task. By writing for the theater (literally or in terms of the theater of the mind), Browning could sidestep the solipsistic dangers of the Romantic exploration of self. By adopting a series of personas, Robert Browning the poet could avoid having to bare his own soul in an obvious manner to the world (a prospect that always filled him with dread). *Pauline* is indeed an autobiographical poem, or at least a poem rooted in autobiographical experiences and the need to comprehend them through art; but it is also true that Browning was trying to distance his poetry from this kind of experience and that drama furnished him with a means of doing so.

If such is the case, then it has to be said he did not succeed. Browning's plan came to nothing: he did write, apparently, a *Pauline, Part 2*, but this was subsequently destroyed. He then suppressed *Pauline* itself, keeping it out of all collected editions of his poetry until 1868, and even then admitting it only "with extreme repugnance." He always regarded the work as something of a failure and assessed it as more or less pretentious. In the 1888 edition of the collected poems, he added a note to the Latin epigraph from Cornelius Agrippa's *De Occulta Philosophia*: "This introduction would appear less absurdly pretentious did it apply, as was intended, to a completed structure of which the poem was meant for only a beginning and remains a fragment." The stress on the fragmentary nature of the work (as, for instance, with the subtitle, "A Fragment of a Confession") may owe something to the Romantic tradition of fragmentary poems (Coleridge's "Kubla Khan," Keats's "Hyperion," and Shelley's "Triumph of Life," among others), and it may hint at the impossibility of complete or whole artistic expression, a theme to which Browning would return. But it is equally possible that Browning stressed the work as a fragment in order to deflect criticism from a work he felt himself to be inadequate.

Although *Pauline* is by no means a perfect poem, it is certainly not as bad as Browning's own reaction suggests. This discrepancy raises the question, Why did Browning feel that his first venture into the realm of published poetry was such a failure?

Three figures act as points of focus for the narrator's somewhat rambling comments and observations. First, there is Pauline herself, the woman with whom the narrator is (it seems) in love and the person to whom the strikingly erotic opening of the poem is addressed:

> Pauline, mine own, bend o'er me—thy soft breast
> Shall pant to mine—bend o'er me—thy sweet eyes,
> And loosened hair, and breathing lips, and arms
> Drawing me to thee—these build up a screen
> To shut me in with thee. (1–5)

But the affair is not as straightforward as these words of desire might suggest, and the narrator's relationships with the two other figures, God and Shelley, provide the poem with much of its content. The narrator of the poem passes, as Browning did, through a period of atheism, but the loss of God precipitates a period of generalized depression. "I have always had one lode-star . . . a yearning after God" (292–295) the narrator announces; without God (a concept replaced with the Shelleyan notion of "Power . . . / Having no part in God" (250–251) his self-consciousness takes him over, and his dreams collapse:

> First went my hopes of perfecting mankind,
> And faith in them—then freedom in itself,
> And virtue in itself—and then my motives' ends,
> And powers and loves; and human love went last. (458–461)

It is Pauline who helps him recover from this nadir, this state of "despair"—"O Pauline! I am ruined," he confesses to her near the beginning of the poem: "my soul had floated . . . into the dim orb / Of self . . . It has conformed itself to that dim orb, / Reflecting all its shades and shapes" (89–94). The bulk of the poem explores this morbid self-obsession, but by the end of the poem Pauline has helped the narrator grow out of the state of selfhood to the point where he can positively address all three chief protagonists. "Love me—love me, Pauline," he entreats, "love nought but me; / Leave me not" (903–904); and right at the end he can address Shelley: "Sun-treader, I believe in God, and truth, / And love" (1020–1021). It seems to be an extremely affirmative note on which to end, as if *Pauline* (like Carlyle's *Sartor Resartus*) traces a journey through the dark night of the soul and into the everlasting yea.

The parallel with Carlyle is appropriate in that, like *Sartor Resartus*, *Pauline* marks the transference from the Romantic to the Victorian, or at least tries to make that mark. But Browning's own attitude to the work suggests that he did not consider the poem in these terms. In fact, a single piece of criticism sunk *Pauline* in Browning's eyes, a piece of criticism that nobody but Browning read, written by a man Browning had never met, and yet a criticism whose impact was so profound that it shaped the entire development of his career.

Unable to find a publisher, Browning had *Pauline* privately printed, using money donated by his aunt. Browning later claimed that not a single copy of this edition was sold. Where reviews were printed, they were mostly very brief and quite dismissive. *Tait's Edinburgh Magazine* reviewed it in a single line: "a piece of utter bewilderment"; and *Fraser's Magazine* described its (anonymous) author as "the Mad Poet of the Batch."[7] But one copy was sent to the eminent man of letters John Stuart Mill for review, with the hope that endorsement from so famous a man would help the poem. Browning did not know Mill personally, but Mill took his duties seriously and copiously annotated his copy with comments and queries. In the end, Mill never got around to actually composing his review, and so the volume was returned to Browning with Mill's comments written all over it.

Mill noted passages he thought beautiful, striking, and true; but in general his comments were severely critical. Browning had hoped that his poem traced a path out of obsessive self-consciousness toward a healthy attitude concerning the world, other people, and God. The poem made an exactly contrary impression on Mill:

The writer seems to me possessed with a more intense and morbid self-consciousness than I ever knew in any sane human being . . . The self-seeking and self-worshipping state is well described—beyond that, I should think the writer had made, as yet, only the next step; viz. into despising his own state . . . he does not write as if it were purged out of him—if he once could muster a hearty hatred of his selfishness, it would *go*—as it is he feels only the *lack of good*, not the positive *evil*.

This must have stung Browning bitterly: he is accused of virtual insanity, certainly of self-obsession. Acting the young, pride-wounded young poet, Browning went through the volume with his own pen in hand, answering Mill's marginal annotations, trying to provide his half of the debate in a silent arena.

Some critics have played down the effect of Mill's remarks on Browning's development as a poet, arguing that *Pauline* can be seen as a straightforward dramatic monologue, in line with the rest of Browning's career.[8] But it seems clear that Browning considered Mill's criticisms very carefully. He had thought he had overcome the dangers of self-consciousness; he had thought he had found a dramatic mode of expression that distanced the poetry from confession. If he was wrong, then perhaps he needed to emphasize the dramatic element more strongly.

Chapter Two

The Experimental Period, 1833–1845: *Paracelsus, Sordello*

I. *Paracelsus*

It is not an easy thing to read through Browning's output chronologically, particularly if one is coming to the poet for the first time. Three difficult and lengthy works—*Pauline*, *Paracelsus*, and *Sordello*—lie between us and the more accessible middle-period work like three great dragons guarding a hoard of gold.[1] Certainly, there is something intimidating about the sheer length of these works (over 11,000 lines of verse in total), to say nothing of the reputation for difficulty and obscurity attached to the third one; and describing them as the products of "The Experimental Period" as I do here may only make matters worse. After all, why should we bother with an author's early experiments when we can skip directly to the mature achievement? It is worth remembering, however, that Browning did not consider himself to be tinkering unsuccessfully with his poetry during this period: each text was set before the world as a completed and self-sufficient work, and there is every reason to believe that he expected each to succeed. As it happened, success was not to come to Browning until the 1860s.

I want to stress the merits of this early work at the beginning of this chapter, because there is a danger that my reading of the work Browning produced between 1833 and 1845 might encourage readers to neglect or dismiss it. This would not only be a shame; it would be an injustice. It is true that, prompted by the various adverse criticisms each subsequent work received, Browning labored to redefine his sense of poetry; during this period Browning was revisionary in both senses of the term—he revised as well as re-envisioned.[2] But this does not mean that there is anything temporary or contingent about the work produced during this period. In fact, some of Browning's best poetry is contained in these poems, and they provide an invaluable sense of Browning's development.

It is highly probable that Browning found Mill's assessment of *Pauline* discouraging. He wrote little for the best part of a year. Instead, he traveled, leaving England for the first time in the company of a family friend, the Chevalier George de Benkhausen, consul general for Russia in England. The Chevalier invited Robert to accompany him on an official journey to St. Petersburg. He was away for three months, and on his return he considered taking up a diplomatic career. It is unclear what Browning's motives for this move were—perhaps he hoped to escape from poetry, or perhaps he was seeking a deeper sense of "real life" to help him write better poetry. He was led to believe that there was a place for him on a diplomatic mission to Persia, but nothing came of this plan.

Browning had written two shorter poems while in Russia, "Porphyria's Lover" and "Johannes Agricola in Meditation." Both are classics, superbly crafted dramatic monologues; and both were successfully published in a journal, the *Monthly Repository*, under the laconic pseudonym "Z." (I discuss these two poems in the next chapter.) Again, with hindsight, it is easy to see these two works as the future for Browning; their brand of short, tightly controlled, and tremendously suggestive poetic monologue is, perhaps, what we most associate with Browning's name today—it represents his most lasting contribution to poetry. But hindsight is a little misleading. Browning did not throw himself into the composition of like pieces. He considered the job of a true poet to be the creation of a long poem, an epic or weighty philosophical masterpiece, and in this (of course) he was not alone in the company of poets, past and present. He decided to try and write a sizable work, taking into account Mill's strictures: something that would explore the development of a soul and be dramatic in principle; an introspective poem, but distanced from "morbid self-consciousness."

For his subject, he settled on the life of the sixteenth-century scholar and alchemist Aureole Theophrastus Bombastus van Hohenstein, called "Paracelsus." The form he decided upon, with Mill in mind, was dramatic, but not the sort of drama that could ever be staged, since *Paracelsus* includes virtually no action and the characters' speeches are sometimes hundreds of lines long. If *Pauline* had appeared too internalized, Browning wanted to make sure that *Paracelsus* be taken as unequivocally externalized. Paracelsus, as both a historical personage and a character in a play, would hopefully not be thought to represent a portrait of Robert Browning. Browning considered this form "novel . . . made after rules of my own, on a subject of my own, in a manner of my own."[3] Actually, several Romantics had produced dramas designed to be read rather than acted, and Shelley's *Prometheus Unbound* immediately strikes the reader as a parallel (although Goethe's *Faust* is probably a closer parallel, given the similarities between the careers of Faust and Paracelsus). But Browning was keen, as his preface makes plain, to identify his production as a poem: "I have endeavoured," he insists, "to write a poem, not a drama," adding that the work depended "on the intelligence and sympathy of the reader for its success—indeed, were my scenes stars it must be his co-operating fancy which, supplying all chasms, shall connect the scattered lights into one constellation."

Browning's *Paracelsus* is only loosely based on the career of the historical figure; its five parts trace a double pattern of "Paracelsus Aspires," "Paracelsus Attains," "Paracelsus," "Paracelsus Aspires," and "Paracelsus Attains." Each scene focuses on the protagonist at a crucial, epiphanic moment of inner realization and expansion: the drama does not articulate external events so much as the development of soul, Paracelsus's mind and spirit. The reason for the repetitive structure should become apparent soon, but the first question is, To what does Paracelsus aspire? And what does he attain?

The short answer is knowledge. The first part finds Paracelsus at home in Würzburg with Festus and Michal, early friends of the thinker who are now man and wife. Paracelsus announces that he will give up his comfortable life and devote himself to the search for some ultimate truth—"the secret of the world— / Of man, and man's true purpose, path and fate" (1.287–288). His friends try to dissuade him, but he is adamant and departs on his quest for this supreme, gnostic knowledge. Part Two is set in Constantinople in the house of a Greek conjurer, fourteen years later. Paracelsus has "attained" a certain degree of knowledge, but nonetheless he feels himself to be a failure, his life "spent and decided, wasted past retrieve" (2.37). Here Paracelsus meets the Shelley-like poet-figure Aprile. The two converse, and we realize that they represent two incomplete opposites of what ought to be a whole. Browning puts key phrases into capitals to underline the point:

> *Paracelsus*: I am
> The mortal who aspired to KNOW—and thou?
> *Aprile*: I would LOVE infinitely, and be loved! (2.343–345)

Paracelsus has sought knowledge at the expense of love; Aprile has devoted himself to love without knowledge. Both have done wrong. Paracelsus has indeed attained that to which he aspired, but in doing so he has discovered that without love his aspirations were incomplete. Aprile, on the other hand, seems to be in a worse state. We discover that he is on the verge of death, and despite Paracelsus's urging ("Die not, Aprile: we must never part. / Are we not halves of one dissevered world?" [2.587–588]) he expires at the end of the section. His final insight (again hammered home with capital letters) is that "God is the PERFECT POET, / Who in his person acts his own creations" (2.601–602).

The third part shows Paracelsus five years later as a professor at the University of Basle, universally famous for his learning. Even Festus, skeptical in the first part, has been converted to a belief in his friend's genius, but Paracelsus is far from happy—he thinks his students are blockheads, despises the life of a teacher, and dwells on his failures. In a reversal of the first part, Festus attempts to convince him of his own genius, but Paracelsus is not to be won over. In the fourth part, Paracelsus has reverted to "aspiring"; he has left (or been kicked out of) the University and now drinks, remembers the past with bitterness, and voices some rather negative opinions—"mind is nothing but disease, / And natural health is ignorance" (4.272–273). The point is that Paracelsus has tried to mediate his search for knowledge with love, but that this has been a mere pretense. To quote Browning's own gloss: "he flings away the mask he has been constrained to wear—does not pretend any longer to love men or care for their love—resolves to continue his pursuit of knowledge, *mere knowledge* . . . He believes Love is extinct in him."[4] His aspiration is as mistaken as it was the first time, but his ultimate attainment, in the final part, is real, because it is prompted not by the search for knowledge, but by the reassertion of love. At the end of Part Four, Paracelsus learns that Michal is dead; the grief he feels convinces him that he is capable of love. The fifth part finds him on his deathbed; he wakes from a fever with a delirious series of memories, but becomes lucid in a lengthy dying speech that distills all the wisdom his experiences have given him (5.583–890). Immediately upon concluding his speech, he dies, deliriously imagining himself "hand in hand with . . . Aprile" (5.893).

As a moral, this may seem a little trite: knowledge must go hand in hand with love, the scientist with the poet; a balanced outlook is paramount. We might, if this were all, say, So what? But, in fact, there is something more profound going on here than might at first appear. The key lies in the precise meanings of these two terms, knowledge and love. Something more specific is meant by these words than the designation of typical dichotomies such as science/art, matter/spirit, and so on. *Knowledge* (we might say, *KNOWLEDGE*) is used in the Gnostic or Platonic sense with which Paracelsus is associated. In this philosophical sense, knowing or gnosis is the aim of the thinker, and the thinker should devote his or her whole life to the quest for it. Moreover, this knowledge is to be found within, quite specifically not in the outside world, whose sensations and appetites function as barriers to transcendent knowing. Something like this philosophy, in an aestheticized form, is behind the thinking of several major Romantics—particularly Blake and Coleridge, in different ways. Certainly the emphasis on the inner life, on the predominance of the imagination, is Romantic.

The other side of the equation is *LOVE*, and by this Browning means a broad empathy and fellowship with all other human beings, not the more narrowly defined romantic love between two people. To adopt this as our philosophy, we must submerge ourself in other people, live and work through and for others, behave in a way we might think of as more in line with Victorian notions of duty and self-sacrifice. I need to be careful here not to crudely schematize these two terms, knowledge and love, as Romanticism and Victorianism: their relationship is more suggestive than that. But what is clear is that knowledge and love are simply not compatible qualities. The one is inward looking and actively requires seekers to alienate themselves from the world (Paracelsus announces that he searches for "an inmost centre of us all, / Where truth abides in fullness" [1.740–741]). The other is by definition gregarious, sympathetic, and requires one to live in the world. After meeting Aprile, Paracelsus decides that he must mix these two, must live actively and lovingly in the world while continuing his search for knowledge. Not surprisingly, he finds this impossible and ends up detesting the students he has to teach. Failing, he replaces the key term in the equation, announcing to Festus, "I seek to KNOW and to ENJOY" (4.236), the enjoyment being chiefly of the sort found in the bottle. But on his deathbed, Paracelsus overcomes his sense of failure. He remembers the death of Aprile, almost hallucinating that the poet is with him now.

> I would have ask'd if he
> KNOWS as he LOVES—if I shall LOVE as well
> As KNOW; but that cold hand, like lead—so cold.
>   (5.115–117)

In his final speech, Paracelsus does attain the realization that these two elements can be brought closer together. But he also comprehends that it is an impossibility for the present. "Paracelsus Attains" for a second time, but whereas Paracelsus had at first indeed believed that truth was something that could be attained—could be grasped, held, encompassed—the use of the term in Part Five is ironic. Paracelsus's insight is that this synthesis, this transcendent truth, exists in God, who is forever just out of reach:

> God tastes an infinite joy
> In infinite ways—one everlasting bliss,
> From whom all being emanates . . .
>   where dwells enjoyment there is He!
> With still a flying point of bliss remote—
> A happiness in store afar—a sphere
> Of distant glory in full view; thus climbs
> Pleasure its heights for ever and for ever. (5.628–637)

Forever climbing, never at the summit. The earlier Paracelsus would have cursed this state of affairs ("Ah, the curse, Aprile, Aprile! / We get so near—so very, very near. / Tis an old tale: Jove strikes the Titans down" [5.119–121]), but in his last hour Paracelsus is able to appreciate it.

His fable about the evolution of the perfect race (5:668–706) has been taken by many, Browning himself in later years, to be a curious foreshadowing of Darwin's later and more famous theory of evolution. In 1881 Browning announced, "all that seems *proved* in Darwin's scheme was a conception familiar to me from the beginning: see in *Paracelsus* the progressive development from senseless matter to organized, until man's appearance (*Part V*)."[5] But in fact, the point of Paracelsus's final speech has less in common with the rationalist-scientific Darwin and more with the mystical ancient philosopher Heracleitus:

> Prognostics told
> Man's near approach; so in man's self arise
> August anticipations, symbols types
> Of a dim splendour ever on before,
> In the eternal circle life pursues. (5.760–764)

This state of continual deferring, the impossibility of "attaining" cou-
pled with the necessity of "aspiring," is perhaps the most central insight
of Browning's poetry. As his Andrea del Sarto was to say nearly twenty
years later, "Ah, but a man's reach should exceed his grasp / Or what's a
heaven for?" (97–98). The perfection that Paracelsus has sought, the
marriage of knowledge and love, can be found only in God ("God is the
PERFECT POET," as Aprile realised). We may not be able to apprehend
God, of course, but we can approach Him, and this process of approaching, the possibility of continual progress, becomes the purpose of life. It
is for this reason that the later Paracelsus decides there is such a thing as
life after death ("I do not believe we wholly die" [4.648]) in order to
allow this process to continue—not, as some critics have suggested,
because his present life is so unsatisfactory.[6] Browning has reimagined
the universe as an environment wherein men and women must continually augment their souls and move closer to a goal they cannot ultimately reach.

Paracelsus was the first of Browning's productions that might be
termed a success. It is true to say that most of the major journals of the
day did not review it, and such reviews as did appear were mixed—the
Athenaeum called it "dreamy and obscure" and deplored the influence of
Shelley, but friends of the poet published positive reviews in the Exam-
iner and the Monthly Repository. Paracelsus made no money (the expenses
of printing it had been met by Browning's father anyway), but it
brought Browning to the attention of a literary circle in London and
gave him a small name as a poet. Indeed, the next nine volumes that
Browning published identified him to the public with the legend "By
the Author of Paracelsus." Browning, meanwhile, had grander plans for
himself.

II. Sordello

Browning had been working on Sordello irregularly throughout the
1830s. Like Paracelsus, Sordello was a historical personage, a thirteenth-
century poet from Provence, who lived in Italy, became involved in politics, and is mentioned in Dante. But as with Paracelsus, Browning's aim
was not to produce a narrative of "the events of Sordello's life" but
rather to trace the development of Sordello's soul and examine (since the
protagonist was a poet) the relationship between the artist and the
world. In other words, Browning did not attempt to lay out Sordello's
biography in his poem. He assumed that his readers would already

know about Sordello's life—that if they did not, they would be able to look him up in any encyclopedia or dictionary of biography. *Sordello* is a text that explores aspects of a life—variations on a theme rather than a bare statement of the theme itself. It is worth dwelling on this point, because although the reputation *Sordello* acquired on publication for impenetrable obscurity has never left it, this is in large part a fault of the way in which the poem is read. If you open a copy of *Sordello* expecting to have everything explained to you, perplexity is the likely result. If, however, you have some sense of Sordello's historical career and an eye to Browning's approach, the text will not be so intractable.

Indeed, the "story" of the poem is quite straightforward. Sordello grows up a sensitive, intense young man in a castle near Mantua. Alienated from the world, he takes solace in the inner life and creates imaginary figures to populate it. So involved is he with the ideal that it only takes one glimpse of the beautiful young noblewoman Palma for him to fall completely in love with her. In fact, the Sordello presented to us in the first book rather resembles the narrator of *Pauline*, or indeed the young Robert Browning himself. In the second book Sordello attends a tournament, or "Court of Love," being held by Palma. The chief poet of the day, Eglamour, is just finishing a song, but Sordello recognizes the work as incomplete, snatches up a harp, and provides his own conclusion. So beautiful is his song that Palma immediately declares him the winner of the contest, and Eglamour, with surprising good grace, lies down and dies. Having chanced upon his career, Sordello becomes not merely a poet but an important citizen and soldier of Mantua. As such, he is caught up in the strife between the two powerful Italian families of Guelf and Ghibbeline. At this point in the poem, Browning departs from the narrative to meditate upon the themes of his work. Most of the third book is a digression set in modern-day Venice, which Browning had visited while researching *Sordello*. In Book Four, we meet Taurello Salinguerra, the great soldier and general who is fighting for the lordly Ghibelines (as opposed to the more liberal Guelphs). Salinguerra is laying siege to Ferrara. Sordello, visiting the siege, learns that Salinguerra is in fact his long-lost father. The general offers his son the chance to rule an Italian empire, and Sordello is faced with the dilemma that characterizes the remainder of the poem: Should he accept worldly power in the hope that he can do some good with it? Or should he stay true to his principles, reject Salinguerra's offer, and attempt something in his own manner? The debate takes up Book Five and most of Book Six, but Sordello's eventual decision—to choose principles over politics, even at the expense of personal power—is rather undermined by the fact that he dies before he is able to do anything further. In other words, Browning is working away at the themes that have fascinated him from the beginning of the 1830s. Sordello demonstrates that while it is not enough to be an inward-gazing Romantic poet, working in the world is likely to dirty your hands.

Browning had spent the best part of seven years composing his epic—writing, revising, rewriting, polishing—and it contains the distillation of his current thoughts on art and life. In all likelihood he expected great things from the reception of *Sordello*. If so, then he must have suffered one of the most complete disappointments in literary history. The poem was published on March 7, 1840, and its author did not have to wait long for disillusionment. On March 14, the *Spectator* published a review:

> What this poem may be in its extent we are unable to say, for we *cannot* read it. Whatever may be the poetical spirit of Mr. Browning, it is so overlaid in *Sordello* by digression, affectation, obscurity, and all the faults that spring, it would seem, from crudity of plan and a self opinion which will neither cull thoughts nor revise composition, that the reader—at least this reader—at least a reader of our stamp—turns away.[7]

One or two reviews were more favorable; most were harsher. "A failure *in toto*," announced the *Monthly Chronicle*; "unintelligible oozings of nonsense," said the *Metropolitan Magazine*. Jane Carlyle, wife of the famous writer and sage, joked that she had read the whole of the poem without ever being able to work out whether Sordello was a man, a city, or a book. Tennyson declared that he had only understood two lines out of the whole work, the first and last ("Who will may hear Sordello's story told" and "Who would has heard Sordello's story told"), and that they were both lies. Charles Macready's diary records his responses to the work: "After dinner tried—another attempt—utterly desperate—on *Sordello*; it is *not* readable." Douglas Jerrold, the playwright, was recovering from a serious illness, and friends bought him a copy of *Sordello* to while away the time of his convalescence. Opening the book, Jerrold turned pale and cried out that he must have lost his wits in his illness, because he was unable to understand two lines of an English poem together.

In fact, the question of obscurity has in many ways hijacked *Sordello*. The chief question the poem has provoked in the minds of most critics relates to the issue of intelligibility. How does the difficulty of *Sordello* relate to its poetic project? Is it, in some sense, a poem *about* obscurity, difficulty? Can Sordello's early alienation from the world and his later decision not to engage in the political arena be the chief theme of the poem? Some critics think so. In fact, it seems very clear to me that these critics are on the wrong track, that "obscurity" is a red herring when it comes to reading *Sordello*. It may seem implausible, but Browning simply did not anticipate his readership (which he acknowledged to be a small one) having any difficulties reading his epic—indeed, he talked about his work as "rather of a more popular nature" (*Correspondence*, 3.134) than his earlier publications. So perhaps the question should be, What went wrong?

Sordello actually explores the same theme that both of Browning's earlier works explore, namely the nature of the interaction between the poet (or thinker) and the world. For Browning, this issue divided itself into two fields that he dramatizes in *Paracelsus* as "Knowledge" and "Love" and that he will later describe in terms of the objective and the subjective. As I have suggested, this dichotomy can be characterized very loosely in terms of Romantic and Victorian ideology—the inward looking, unitary vision on the one hand (with its dangers of solipsism and alienation) and the outward looking, self-abnegating sense of duty on the other (which, by itself, leads one entirely away from the necessary power of the imagination).

The young Sordello lives entirely for love, much as Aprile did in *Paracelsus*. He is raised in isolation, with only a few servants for company:

> Some foreign women-servants, very old,
> Tended and crept about him—all his clue
> To the world's business and embroiled ado
> Distant a dozen hill-tops at the most.
> Art first a simple sense of life engrossed
> Sordello in his drowsy Paradise. (1.622–627)

Alone, Sordello "contrives / A crowd" (1.747–748) from his imagination, and he lives entirely in this world. The dangers of this self-absorption are obvious; and when Sordello first sees Palma he does not respond to her as another human being, but rather integrates her into his imaginary world as his Perfect Woman—the Daphne to his Apollo. Sordello is living in the "bubble of fancy," as Browning describes it in the running headnotes he added to the poem in 1863 (to help elucidation). But *Sordello* the poem traces a trajectory from this one extreme to its complete opposite: Sordello is offered not just a place in the world, but *the* place—he is given the chance not just to live among men and women, but to rule over them as King. He goes, in the fullest sense, from love to knowledge—or, more precisely, from subjective to objective, from existing with reference only to the One above, to devoting his life to the many below.

Sordello is structured on the transition from the one state of being to the other. The first two books concentrate on Sordello's life in the subjective mode. The last two books interrogate the choice he is offered to partake of the objective mode. The third book, as I noted, consists mostly of a giant digression in which Browning discusses the role poetry should have in relation to life. To suggest that he advocates compromise misrepresents his argument; compromise sounds rather wet and ineffectual. In fact, Browning demonstrates an acute awareness of human suffering and a similar appreciation of the relative ineffectiveness of poetry to relieve the bulk of human misery. But poetry in its fullest, Shelleyan sense is still of vital centrality to life, as Browning conceives it. Book Four, with its detailed descriptions of the horrors inflicted on people by war (in this case, the siege of Ferrara) reinforces this theme; and it is the sight of this suffering that profoundly alters Sordello's own outlook.

The eventual death of Sordello is similar to the death of Paracelsus. Both characters seek a perfect integration—in Sordello's case, a resurrection of the ideal Roman republic, in which the inward life of the poet could be balanced against the outward life of the helper of mankind. But both characters ultimately comprehend that their ideals are unrealizable—at least in this world. As his life collapses under the pressure of reconciling the opposites (his "flesh-half's break-up"), Sordello has, however, an epiphanic revelation, a "closing-truth":

> So seemed Sordello's closing-truth evolved
> By his flesh-half's break-up; the sudden swell
> Of his expanding soul showed Ill and Well,
> Sorrow and Joy, Beauty and Ugliness,
> Virtue and Vice, the Larger and Less,
> All qualities, in fine, recorded here,

Might but be modes of Time, . . .

. . . but not force to bind

Eternity. (6.466–474)

For this reason Sordello decides, as Paracelsus had decided, that there must be a life after death: because only in an afterlife freed from time can these apparently unreconcilables be placed in a proper and harmonious relation. Sordello's death (he dies of the stress of his conflicting loyalties at the end of the sixth book), then, like Paracelsus's, is not wholly a tragic occurrence. He is able to continue with the evolution of his soul toward God after life, although the narrator of *Sordello* suggests that his decision not to accept the opportunity for political power was a mistake—"the one step too mean / For him to take—we suffer at this day / Because of" (6.830–832). The Shelleyan mode of *Alastor* has been enacted again; the poet has died in solipsistic mode, and mankind has gone on suffering.

III. Browning's "Obscurity"

The fact remains that Browning's epic, his most complete poetic statement to date, was greeted with virtual howls of derision and noncomprehension. It seems clear that Browning was deeply hurt by the almost unanimous condemnation—he wrote ruefully to his friend Fanny Haworth that critics had been pelting *Sordello* with "cabbage stump after potato-paring" (*Correspondence*, 4.269). But the question remains, How could Browning fail to anticipate the reception his poem would face? There seems to be some gap between Browning's sense of what constituted poetry and what his readership expected.

As I have suggested, the chief difficulty is stylistic. The plot of *Sordello* is straightforward—if one were troubled only by (to reiterate Jane Carlyle's bon mot) an inability to determine the physical identity of Sordello, that matter could be easily rectified with a five-minute recourse to any encyclopedia. But the major problem facing Browning's readership was then, and perhaps still is today, readability. "Unintellible oozings of nonsense": this sentiment, or one quite like it, recurs again and again in contemporary reviews of Browning's publications. Browning's style was, many claimed, a type of poetic gobbledygook. A reviewer of *Dramatic Lyrics* (1842) declared that this was Browning's overriding fault:

The inaptitude for giving intelligible expression to his meanings, whether unconscious or artificial, whether its cause be affectation or incapacity, is a defect, lessening the value in any available sense, of the meanings themselves.[8]

Some light is thrown on this question by an exchange of letters between Browning and one of his later friends, John Ruskin, the art critic and writer. Ruskin had been sent a copy of *Men and Women* shortly after its publication, and on December 2, 1855, he wrote to thank the donor. But he also confessed that he had been having difficulties interpreting some of the poems ("I don't understand at all!!!!!!!").[9] After discussing one of Browning's more challenging poems ("Popularity"), Ruskin goes on,

> Your Ellipses are quite Unconscionable: before one can get through ten lines, one has to patch you up in twenty places, wrong or right, and if one hasn't much stuff of one's own to spare to patch with! You are worse than the worst Alpine Glacier I ever crossed. Bright, & deep enough truly, but so full of Clefts that half the journey has to be done with ladder & hatchet. However, I have found some great things in you already, and I think you must be a wonderful mine, when I have real time & strength to set to work properly.

The image of Browning as a sort of polar landscape is certainly striking—bright and deep but hard work to traverse. But Ruskin's preconceptions about poetry are also clear: he assumes that a poet should make everything in his or her poetry quite plain and lucid and that a reader ought not be expected to contribute to the process of deriving meaning ("patching up" the ellipses). Underneath is an unspoken conviction that "meaning" is something straightforward and stable, that Browning could, if he chose, render this "meaning" in a direct manner. Browning, in his reply, points out that Ruskin and he have radically different conceptions of poetry:

> We don't read poetry the same way, by the same law; it is too clear. I cannot begin writing poetry till my imaginary reader has conceded licences to me which you demur at altogether. I *know* that I don't make out my conception by my language, all poetry being a putting the infinite within the finite. You would have me paint it all plain out, which can't be; but by various artifices I try to make shift with touches and bits of outlines which *succeed* if they bear the conception from me to you. You ought, I think, to keep pace with the thought tripping from ledge to

ledge of my "glaciers," as you call them; not stand poking your alpen-stock into the holes, and demonstrating that no foot could have stood there;—suppose it sprang over there?

"All poetry being a putting the infinite within the finite." Most critics have taken this phrase as the closest Browning came to articulating a central aesthetic tenet.[10] But just as important as this rather abstract notion is the phrase that precedes it: "I don't make out my conception by my language." Fundamental questions of language underlie the mat-ter of Browning's difficult style. As far as Browning is concerned, expe-rience simply cannot be represented in language in a straightforward, lucid way. Language is not up to the task—or, to put it less negatively, experience is too large, too awkward and intractable, to be transferred into a linguistic frame. This is particularly true of all three of Browning's first publications; Browning might argue that it is simply impossible for any selection of words to thoroughly and comprehensively capture or apprehend his subject ("Soul," or the complexities of mind in its rela-tions to the world)—because ultimately the subject is divine, therefore infinite, and therefore beyond understanding in human language. The most a poet can do is move toward such a subject, to set in motion in the mind of the reader the process of interpretation that is behind the poems themselves. Language works by provoking processes of interpre-tation in the reader; writing is not the pristine passage of a notion from the writer's imagination directly into the reader's mind. Texts come into being through a process of working out.

Sordello himself faces this problem when he begins writing poetry:

> The first trial was enough:
> He left imagining, to try the stuff
> That held the imaged thing and, let it writhe
> Never so fiercely, scarce allowed a tithe
> To reach the light—his Language. (2.569–573)

In other words, his "first trial" as a poet is the discovery that language, "the stuff / That held the imaged thing" actually captured only a frac-tion (a "tithe") of his imaginings. Sordello's response is to invent a new language, and we are told how he "re-wrought / That Language" into a fitter vehicle. Browning himself embarked on a similar endeavor, and the style of *Sordello*, the style that so offended the reviewers, was part of the solution. The point here, something that Browning's letter to Ruskin makes plain, is the way the style draws the reader into the process of interpretation. A reader of Browning must "concede licences to him"; in particular he or she must actively work at the poem and not expect to be carried along effortlessly. This sort of style is, properly, not obscure: it is always possible to work toward meaning once we understand that part of the meaning derives from us ("right or wrong," as Ruskin anxiously pointed out). It is a style that suggests rather than declares, that opens up avenues of signification rather than closing them down. What the hostile reviews of *Sordello* actually demonstrate is an unwillingness to undertake the arduous labors involved in actively working out the meaning of a six-book, densely written epic poem. And that, we might say, is something we can understand.

Chapter Three
The Dramatic Monologue

By the early 1840s Browning had not yet discovered a satisfactory poetic form. He had tried writing in a Shelleyan mode (*Pauline*), but according to Mill the result was too morbidly self-conscious for sanity. He had tried writing a philosophical poetic-drama (*Paracelsus*), with some success, although the whole was rather dry and static. He then tried his hand at epic (*Sordello*), but the mocking response of readers and critics told him that this was not a successful development of his art. I have been arguing that Browning was deliberately trying to come to terms with the reactions of his audiences. He continually revised his poetic project, attempting to reconcile what he knew to be contradictories—the subjective and objective, the Romantic heritage and the Victorian imperative. Romantic thesis and Victorian antithesis would eventually lead to a synthesis in the form we know today as the dramatic monologue, but the pathway Browning took toward this happy development was more purely dramatic.

I. Browning's Plays and *Pippa Passes*

Browning's introduction to the world of drama came via the theatrical impresario Charles Macready. Macready, always on the lookout for new material to perform at his Covent Garden playhouse, asked Browning to write a play. Browning replied with *Strafford*. Despite his reservations about the play's lack of dramatic power, Macready was true to his word, and Browning's first play was staged at Covent Garden on May 1, 1837. It managed five performances before closing by the end of the month.

Browning went on to write four more plays for performance, but none of them were successes. Macready refused to stage all but one; and the one he did not reject (*A Blot in the 'Scutcheon*, 1843, which he staged unwillingly at Dickens's insistence) closed after three nights. Browning, by any standard criterion, was a failure as a dramatist.

The basic problem with Browning's plays is their predominance of character and a corresponding lack of action. Three hours in a theater watching various actors deliver lengthy speeches unleavened by any-

31

thing actually happening is a dispiriting experience. But Browning's artistic credo, as the preface to *Strafford* makes clear (and as we might perhaps have guessed from *Paracelsus* and *Sordello*) is "Action in Character rather than Character in Action." Browning was true to his interest in the development of soul, the inner narrative, rather than to public interest in the plotting of external events. On the other hand we can also see why Browning was drawn to drama in the first place. Playwriting provided objective form for subjective exploration. It guarded against the pitfalls of Shelleyan lyric—excessive introspection, solipsism—by ensuring a certain detachment. Drama, it seems, was a necessary intermediate form in Browning's development.

Browning's flirtation with the theater, however ill-starred it seems in retrospect, lasted nearly a decade and was still shaping Browning's sense of himself in 1855, a fact demonstrated by the conclusion to "A Light Woman" (a poem from *Men and Women*):

> Well, any how, here the story stays,
> So far at least as I understand;
> And Robert Browning, you writer of plays,
> Here's a subject made to your hand! (53–56)

Of course, there is a wry sense of his lack of success as a dramatist in this allusion, but nonetheless Browning seems to be regarding himself as primarily a playwright. In fact, "A Light Woman" gives us a good clue as to the timbre of Browning's half-a-dozen plays. The poem concerns a coquette. The narrator of the poem is worried that his friend will fall into her clutches, so with the aim of extricating him from her coils he courts her himself. He, of course, is not in love with her; but too late he realizes that the seemingly "light woman" has, in fact, fallen in love with him. She has given him her heart, and clearly he is going to break it. The poem ends with the narrator contemplating a situation in which none of the three parties can be called happy. This is the sort of unsatisfactory state of affairs, it seems, that Browning evidently considered typical of his plays.

There is not space here to discuss Browning's dramatic works in any detail, but we can perhaps notice the appositeness of the self-assessment in "A Light Woman." *Strafford*, the first of Browning's plays, is a historical drama tracing the career of Charles the First's general the eponymous Earl of Strafford. The tragedy of the central figure derives not from a fatal flaw but something rather the reverse. Due to his sense of personal honor as well as political and personal sympathies, Strafford is consistently loyal to his king; he is rigorously fair-minded, scrupulously honest, and—in the circumstances of the English Civil War—doomed. The Puritan William Pym, opposing the king, attacks Strafford; King Charles himself is too weak to defend him. The plays ends with Strafford's execution. But the irony of the situation is that it is Strafford's strengths that determine his tragic status rather than his weaknesses, his virtues rather than his vices. It is perhaps too much to describe this worldview as cynical, although, as in "A Light Woman," the situation is certainly ironic.

This consciousness of the irony inherent in everyday life recurs throughout Browning's drama. We can sense it in *King Victor and King Charles* (1842), in *The Return of the Druses* (1843), in the cocktail of carnal love and idealizing passion that underpins *A Blot in the 'Scutcheon* (1843), and in the triumph of the worldly Ogniben in *A Soul's Tragedy* (1846). Most of all, it is present as a continual and subverting undercurrent in *Pippa Passes*, a play that has been (erroneously) cited as embodying Browning's unalloyed optimism.

Pippa Passes emerged as the first publication in a series that carries the rather cryptic title *Bells and Pomegranates*. In a letter of April 7, 1840, we find Browning approaching the publisher William Smith:

> Sir,
>   Mr Moxon has just published a long Poem of mine, "Sordello", meant for a limited class of readers—and I am on the point of following it up by three new Dramas, written in a more popular style, and addressed to the public at large: . . . I mean that these Dramas should form one publication of the same size and at the same low price as your other pamphlets. (*Correspondence*, 4.267)

Browning later told Elizabeth Barrett Browning that the title for this series of cheap pamphlets was a Biblical reference: "The Rabbis make Bells & Pomegranates symbolical of Pleasure and Profit, the Gay & the Grave, the Poetry and the Prose, Singing and Sermonising."[1] The preface Browning wrote for *Pippa Passes*, as the first of this series, explains his populist hopes (although the preface was not, in the end, used):

> Two or three years ago I wrote a Play [*Strafford*], about which the chief matter I much care to recollect at present is, that a Pit-full of goodnatured people applauded it:—ever since, I have been desirous of doing

something in the same way that should better reward their attention. What follows I mean for the first of a series of Dramatical Pieces, to come out at intervals, and I amuse myself by fancying that the cheap mode in which they appear will for once help me to a sort of Pit-audience again.

Browning's hope for a large and wide-ranging audience was not to be fulfilled by *Bells and Pomegranates*, but *Pippa Passes* at least sees him moving in the direction of popularity. True, there is little action as such; but there is certainly variety—four separate one-act playlets, linked together by the connecting device of Pippa passing each of them in turn. The playlets are in differing styles, and the connecting material constitutes some of Browning's most accessible and pleasing lyrics. It is not a play designed to be staged, but it is easy to read, and it invites a sort of internalised, mental performance.

Pippa, the heroine, is a poor orphan girl who works in a silk factory in the northern Italian town of Asolo. *Pippa Passes* represents her single day's holiday, when she wanders happily about the town, singing cheerful songs. As she walks along, her songs intrude on the lives of four sets of people, all wrapped up in their own plans and schemes. In each of the scenes, the tone and action are profoundly changed when the characters overhear Pippa's innocent chants. Evil plotters become conscious-stricken; a husband about to discard his wife changes his mind; a wavering political radical ready to give up his plan to assassinate the Austrian tyrant hears Pippa singing and finds his resolve renewed.

In each case, the poetic merit of Pippa's songs is not something intrinsic but something that derives from their context. Poetry, for Browning, depends as much upon its audience as its composer; it is the balance between the (subjective) latter and the (objective) former that is paramount. Pippa's much-anthologized first song provides an example:

> The year's at the spring,
> And day's at the morn:
> Morning's at seven;
> The hill-side's dew-pearled:
> The lark's on the wing,
> The snail's on the thorn;
> God's in his heaven—
> All's right with the world! (1.215–222)

The optimism of the final couplet epitomized Browning's worldview for a whole generation of critics, but its banality should alert us. We need to be aware who the speaker is—in this case a young girl whose innocence verges on naïveté—and we also need to understand the context in which the text is "spoken." Here, the lyric comes at the end of a scene in which a woman (Ottima) and her lover (Sebald) are rejoicing at having killed her husband. The two of them celebrate their crime: "I crown you / My great white queen," Sebald tells Ottima, "my spirit's arbitress"; he is about to add "magnificent in sin" when they hear Pippa's singing. The mode here, clearly, is not optimism but irony. All is *not* right with the world, as Ottima and Sebald's story shows; quite possibly, God is not in his heaven. Pippa's innocence looks more like ignorance.

Browning's "optimism," like his "obscurity," is something of a red herring; but it would be as much of an error to go to the other extreme and suggest that Browning's poetry advances the notion that all's *wrong* with the world. Throughout his career Browning was wary of absolutes and drawn to the shades of experience, moral or religious. His perspective is that nobody has the complete picture (except, perhaps, God, and He is inaccessible to us); therefore nobody can understand, or judge, wholly and completely. The gap between our religious sense of perfection, the absolute, and our practical experience of this flawed world is what German Romanticist critic Friedrich von Schlegel gave the name "Romantic Irony." According to Schlegel, the true poet uses this discrepancy, this "irony," as a creative motor. He or she makes the reader aware that no work of art can be "perfect" or complete; and features such as self-parody, stylistic roughness, and what later critics would call "alienation techniques" are to be endorsed since they make clear the superiority of (perfect) spirit over (imperfect) world. Browning's conception of the subjective/objective dialectic owes something to Schlegel's views, and Schlegel's particular aesthetic use of the word *irony*, as well as the ordinary meaning of the word, has applications for Browning's art. *Pippa Passes* is an ironic work in both senses.

II. The Dramatic Monologue

The dramatic monologue is probably Browning's most significant contribution to the history of poetry, and in retrospect we can see the blending of lyric and dramatic (of subjective and objective) that it entails as a natural function of Browning's development. It was an attempt to combine the psychological portraiture necessary for the exploration of soul with a dramatic perspective and objectivity that would guard against introspection.

Seeing the dramatic monologue in these terms might suggest that this genre was wholly Browning's invention, the culmination of a particular and personal set of circumstances. However, this would misrepresent the poetic environment that gave rise to Browning's dramatic monologues.[2] Indeed, any number of pre-Victorian poems might, it can be argued, be seen as dramatic monologues—Burns's "Holy Willie's Prayer," the Old English poem *The Wanderer*, Horace's *Epistles*. But there is some point in limiting our use of the term to examples from the nineteenth century and after. There is something distinctly post-Romantic in the psychological portraiture and concentration on the landscape of the mind that we particularly associate with the modern dramatic monologue.

Park Honan's definition of the term "dramatic monologue" is, perhaps, the pithiest: "a single discourse by one whose presence is indicated by the poet but who is not the poet himself."[3] I would add that dramatic monologues are poems about states of mind; they delineate an inner landscape. In our post-Freud era, the dramatic monologue's mode of psychological analysis is commonplace. But in the 1830s, it was very far from so. The bulk of the *Bells and Pomegranates* pamphlets contain Browning's dramatic writing, whether intended for the stage or not. But two, *Dramatic Lyrics* (1842) and *Dramatic Romances and Lyrics* (1845), are collections of shorter works, and it is here that we find Browning's earliest dramatic monologues. It seems likely, as I suggest above, that Browning was working on these shorter poems throughout the late 1830s and into the 1840s. "Dramatic Lyric" looks, at first sight, like a contradiction in terms, but in the context of Browning's development we can see in it a determination to blend the apparently contradictory qualities of drama and lyric.

In fact, Browning and Tennyson seem to have "invented" the dramatic monologue at more or less the same time. While Browning was writing "Porphyria's Lover" on his trip to Russia in 1834, Tennyson was writing a curiously similar poem about religious mania, "Saint Simeon Stylites," in 1833. Neither poet was in touch with the other at this stage in their careers, which makes their contemporaneous "invention" of the form a rather striking coincidence. One explanation is that Romanticism had encouraged poets to concentrate on their inner landscapes; the immediately post-Romantic poets such as Tennyson and Browning approached this notion with a more Victorian desire to be objective about what they saw. The dramatic monologue became the chief means by which Victorian writers anatomized the mind; indeed, some critics have argued that it helped prepare the ground for modern-day psychiatry.[4] But Browning's determination to display the workings of psychotic and insane consciousness was striking, perhaps shocking, to his contemporaries. Added to the evidence of obscurity and affectation (*Sordello* cast a long shadow over Browning's reputation), it was enough to condemn the poet in many eyes. Richard Simpson, writing in the *Rambler*, went so far as to accuse him of being a sort of pig: "We detect a keen enjoyment of dirt as such, a poking of the nose into dunghills and the refuse of hospitals . . . accompanied by the peculiar grunt which expresses not only the pleasure experienced but also the nature of the experiencer."[5]

Herbert Tucker notes "the enormous range of Browning's dramatic lyrics" and suggests that a list of "only the broadest categories" must include "themes of nature, history, art, religion, and love."[6] This is true; Browning is nothing if not a varied poet. Yet at the same time, most of Browning's earliest dramatic monologues can be grouped under a single heading. What they have in common is a fascination with extreme states of mind, a fascination that was to stay with Browning all of his life. Indeed, "extreme states of consciousness" is something of a euphemism. With poems such as "Porphyria's Lover," "Johannes Agricola in Meditation," "Soliloquy of the Spanish Cloister," and "My Last Duchess" we are in fact dealing with sheer insanity.

"Porphyria's Lover," Browning's earliest dramatic monologue, is usefully representative (although insofar as it lacks a specific historical setting it is also unusual for a Browning dramatic monologue). The unnamed narrator seems to love Porphyria; certainly she loves him: "murmuring how she loved me," she vows to "give herself to me forever" (21–25). But the only way the narrator can see to capture this precious moment of intimacy and preserve it forever is to murder Porphyria.

> That moment she was mine, mine, fair,
> Perfectly pure and good: I found
> A thing to do, and all her hair
> In one long yellow string I wound
> Three times her little throat around,
> And strangled her. (36–41)

The narrator is a madman, but he acts not from evil or vicious intentions but from a desire to capture a perfect moment and hold it forever. Out of this apparent contradiction, this irony, Browning constructs something more than just a portrait of a killer. The narrator of "Porphyria's Lover" functions in the same way an artist does: he attempts to immortalize an otherwise fleeting beautiful instant. That he does this without considering the feelings of Porphyria herself can be read as a comment on the dehumanizing tendency of artists to treat others as objects, to disregard their feelings in the service of art. Browning particularly disapproved of this kind of behavior in art as in life, and such artists (there are many of them in Browning's work) are always treated critically.

The interesting, unsettled textual nature of "Porphyria's Lover" includes another aspect, in that we cannot be certain whether the narrator is describing events that really happened, or only relating a deranged fantasy. The narrator describes murdering Porphyria, insisting that "she felt no pain / I am quite sure she felt no pain." Then he goes on:

> As a shut bud that holds a bee,
>   I warily oped her lids: again
>   Laughed the blue eyes without a stain.
> And I untightened next the tress
>   About her neck; her cheek once more
> Blushed bright beneath my burning kiss. (43–48)

He is wary when reopening the dead woman's eyes because he is expecting—what? The metaphorical bee sting of a rebuke? If so, he does not find it. Indeed, the dead Porphyria seems precisely as beautiful and loving as she had been when alive. More so, in fact, because she now has had her "utmost will": she is free of the vicissitudes of existence; she will never grow old. As the narrator remarks at the close, even God is not displeased by his actions ("And all night long we have not stirred, / And yet God has not said a word!"). It is as if Porphyria has passed peacefully into a different, better mode of existence.

But, of course, she did nothing of the sort. She was strangled, a violent and traumatic death. Although the narrator clearly thinks of this murder as an almost noble activity, we as readers can simultaneously comprehend his point of view and see beyond it (read between the lines, as it were) to a much less salubrious reality. Realistically, there is no way a victim of death by strangulation could look the way the narrator describes Porphyria as looking. He talks of "blue eyes without a stain" when in fact the eyes of a strangled woman would be bulging and bloodshot. He mentions untying the tourniquet from around her neck and watching her cheek "blush" under his kisses. But a dead person's blood does not flow; there would be no blush. Had the narrator done what he claims to have done, the situation would not conform to his description.

We might put this down to Browning's ignorance of postmortem appearances (although Browning had at one stage considered a medical career); but it doesn't take much more than common sense to realize that what the narrator describes in lines 43–48 is an idealized rather than a realistic portrait. The key here is that in any dramatic monologue we only have the words of the narrator to go on; consequently, we have to make a choice whether to believe him or her, or not. The suggestion here is that "Porphyria's Lover" describes not a murder but the fantasy of an unhinged mind, a fiction.

Browning's dramatic monologues function on at least two levels simultaneously; they are, to appropriate a term from twentieth-century criticism, dialogic. The act of understanding them compels us to first see things from the point of view of the narrator and then to see the possibilities behind the narrator's words. The text has to be decoded, not in the baffling manner of *Sordello*, but in the same way that we "decode" any speech act. We engage with the poem in working out what it means, imaginatively entering into its world, which is what Browning had wanted from the beginning of his poetic career.

Other poems from *Dramatic Lyrics* require a similar interpretive approach. "Johannes Agricola in Meditation" is exactly the same length and has the same rhyme scheme as "Porphyria's Lover" (in fact, the two poems were originally paired as "Madhouse Cells, 1 & 2"). Here, the speaker is suffering from a form of religious mania, antinomianism, familiar in Britain through the doctrine of predestination advocated by the Scottish Calvinist religion. According to this doctrine, God has known since the beginning of time which people will go to heaven and which to hell. Consequently, those whose name is on the list of the "saved" (those touched by grace) will go to heaven regardless of how many sins they commit, and those who are not will go to hell no matter how good they are. This particular belief had been the subject of literary satire on many previous occasions—in particular, Browning may have been influenced by two Scottish works: Robert Burns's "Holy Willie's Prayer" (1799; this poem can, as mentioned, be seen as a pre-dramatic monologue) and James Hogg's *Confessions of a Justified Sinner* (1824). Johannes Agricola believes himself to be "in God's breast" and to have been there since the beginning of things: "Ere stars were thundergirt, or piled / The heavens . . . God thought on me his child, / Ordained a life for me" (13–16). He feels he can do no wrong:

> I have God's warrant, could I blend
>   All hideous sins, as in a cup,—
> To drink the mingled venoms up,
> Secure my nature will convert
>   To draught to blossoming gladness fast. (33–37)

Again, as in "Porphyria's Lover," we are alerted to the problematic nature of the speaker's claims by internal contradictions. In "Johannes Agricola in Meditation," these are mostly temporal. For example, he says at the beginning, "I intend to get to God, . . . / For 'tis to God I speed so fast" (6–7), but almost immediately he asserts that he is already with God: "I lie—where I have always lain" (11). Throughout the poem, Agricola mixes tenses—future ("I intend to," "could I"), present ("I lie," "I gaze below"), and past ("having thus created me"). The narrator starts the poem down, looking up ("There's Heaven above . . . / I look right through its gorgeous roof" [1–2]); but later he is up, looking down (in God's breast "I gaze below on Hell's fierce bed" [43]). In other words, we are being shown the contours of Agricola's wish-fulfilment; the narrator no sooner gives voice to a thought than he convinces himself that it has already come to pass. As with the narrator of "Porphyria's Lover," we see things from Agricola's point of view and simultaneously place it in perspective, are aware of its limitations.

The process of moving the reader to both empathize with and distance him- or herself from the narrator is particularly well exemplified by "My Last Duchess," one of Browning's most famous monologues. Robert Langbaum's landmark study of the dramatic monologue, *The Poetry of Experience* (1957), explores this poem at length. Langbaum describes this double-edged aspect of the dramatic monologue in terms of sympathy and judgment. Sympathy is required if we are to understand the narrator and what he (or she, but usually he) is concerned about; judgment is necessary because we become aware that the speaker is not telling the whole story, that (for instance) he has done something we need to distance ourselves from, perhaps something we need to criticize.

"My Last Duchess" has unmistakable parallels with the other poems we have been looking at. Like Agricola, the Duke is convinced of his innate superiority and worth. Like Porphyria's lover, he has sought to capture and completely control a fleeting moment by killing a woman. The monologue is part of a discussion the Duke is having with the envoy of a certain Count about the prospect of marrying the Count's daughter. He now shows a portrait of his last wife to the envoy and tells her story. The envoy is curious about the strange expression, the "spot of joy" on the young woman's face. The Count explains, "Sir, 'twas not / Her husband's presence only, called that spot / Of joy into the Duchess' cheek":

> She had
> A heart . . . how shall I say? . . . too soon made glad,
> Too easily impressed; she liked whate'er
> She looked on and her looks went everywhere. (13–24)

The Duke was jealous and gave orders to have his wife eliminated. The poem concludes with him following this bombshell revelation with an affable invitation to "go / Together down," pointing out other interesting objets d'art on the way. The Duke prefers the portrait of his wife to the woman herself; she was, he says, flighty (by which we understand that she was vital and subject to the fluctuations and alterations of life). The picture is static, will never change, and is something over which the Duke, as he is keen to point out, has sole and complete control: "None puts by / The curtain I have drawn for you, but I" (9–10).

In order to understand the poem, we need to sympathize with the Duke. It is possible, I suppose, to wholly sympathize with him, but as this would make us complicit murderers it is clearly not a desirable option. On the other hand, we may (of course) simply condemn the Duke. But as Langbaum argues, "condemnation [is] the least interesting response."[7] We are drawn into the poem by the sheer panache of the Duke's evil. In fact, Langbaum argues, we neither accept nor condemn outright, but combine both responses. The poem works via a tension between sympathy and judgment, a playing off of the two terms against one another. Critics have argued as to whether we should regard the Duke as "witless" for having inadvertently confessed to being a mur-

derer before a servant or as "shrewd" for the cunning way he manipu-
lates the situation.[8] The assessment of the Duke will undoubtedly
depend upon the individual reader. It is likely that he or she will base a
judgment on the terms the Duke actually uses to describe the way he
dealt with the Duchess:

> Oh, Sir, she smiled, no doubt,
> Whene'er I passed her; but who passed without
> Much the same smile? This grew; I gave commands;
> Then all smiles stopped together. There she stands
> As if alive. (43–47)

The implication is that the Duke had the Duchess killed. Much later in
his life, Browning was asked for more information on the fate of the
Duchess:

> He replied meditatively, "Yes, I meant that the commands were that she
> be put to death." And then, after a pause, he added, with a characteristic
> dash of expression, and as if the thought had just started up in his mind,
> "Or he might have had her shut up in a convent."[9]

I think this anecdote is central to the interpretation of Browning's work.
It is not indicative of muddle on the poet's part; rather it recognizes that
once the poem is published, Browning has no more right to impose a
particular reading on the text than any other reader. The ambiguity
inherent in many of Browning's monologues, the way that key interpretive clues can be read in different ways, is of central importance to the
way his poetry works. These texts involve us in the process of interpretation. They open up significance rather than closing it down; they suggest rather than dictate. Browning's is a poetry of becoming rather than
of being. Once this process has been set in motion, not even the poet
himself can stop it.

In the "Soliloquy of the Spanish Cloister" we are given little overt
information. The title tells us that the speaker is a monk in a Spanish
monastery; the poem itself tells us that the speaker nurses an implacable
hatred for a mild-mannered fellow monk, Friar Lawrence. Beyond this
we know practically nothing. Why does the (unnamed) speaker so hate
Lawrence? ("If hate killed men, Brother Lawrence, / God's blood, would
not mine kill you!" [3–4]). What is the larger context for the mono-

logue? What is the precise relation between the two men? We sense that
the motives the narrator provides for himself are insufficient to account
for the violence of his emotions:

> Hell dry you up with its flames!
> At the meal we sit together:
> 　*Salve tibi*! I must hear
> Wise talk of the kind of weather,
> 　Sort of season, time of year. (9–12)

Finally, of course, what matters is less the reason for the narrator's
astonishing outpouring of venom and more the sheer, infectious enthusiasm of it. But the urge to pin the poem down has been too powerful
for whole generations of critics to resist. The last stanza has been particularly motivating; in it the narrator debates whether to pledge his
soul to the devil in order to gain the power to properly torment
Lawrence:

> Or, the Devil!—one might venture
> 　Pledge one's soul yet slily leave
> Such a flaw in the indenture
> 　As he'd miss till, past retrieve,
> Blasted lay that rose-acacia
> 　We're so proud of! *Hy, Zy, Hine . . .*
> St, there's Vespers! *Plena gratia*
> 　*Ave, Virgo*! G-r-r-r- you swine! (65–72)

The general sense is clear: the narrator is prepared to hazard his own
soul (he is apparently oblivious to the risk, here as elsewhere in the
poem) in order to achieve the remarkably petty act of destroying one of
Lawrence's plants. But three words in line 70—"*Hy, Zy, Hine*"—have
spawned almost an entire critical industry by themselves. Dozens of
articles and suggestions in scholarly texts have tried to explain them,
offering a bewildering variety of incompatible suggestions. Are these
words meant to indicate the sound of vesper bells? Are they inconsequential mutterings of the narrator, on a par with "G-r-r-r-"? Are they
words from a medieval parody of the mass? Are they the beginning of
an invocation to the devil?

It is easy to say that critics who have argued this issue back and forth are misplacing their critical energies. The meaning should not be found in pedantic details but rather in the broad sweep of violent emotion that the poem represents. But it is also true that the poem makes a point of pedantry. The narrator himself is a fearful pedant. Brother Lawrence comes across as harmless and open; he is not bothered by minute particulars provided the heart is in the right place. The narrator is otherwise, as his observations about mealtimes make plain:

> When he finishes refection
>   Knife and fork across he lays
> Never to my recollection,
>   As I do, in Jesu's praise
> I the Trinity illustrate,
>   Drinking watered orange-pulp—
> In three sips the Arian frustrate;
>   While he drains his at one gulp. (33–40)

The idea that a man whose heart is so lacking in Christian love can consider himself more devout than the benign Lawrence simply because he places his knife and fork in the shape of a cross at the end of a meal is, of course, ridiculous. But it precisely articulates the character of the narrator as an obsessive religious pedant. The scholars who think that the way to give a critical account of this poem is to interpret *"Hy, Zy, Hine"* or tell us "the Greek name for Swine's Snout" (a question the narrator poses in the poem, [16]), while ignoring the overall sweep of passion, are acting in a manner entirely appropriate to the narrator of this dramatic monologue.

The general point is one of engagement; either we enter imaginatively into the world of the dramatic monologues, or else they are not working properly. It is meaningful for a reader to be caught up in the Spanish Cloister soliloquizer's passionate narrow-mindedness to the extent of thinking the whole work hinges on the significance of three puzzling words near the end. It would be equally meaningful to respond to the poem in other ways (within certain textually determined limits, of course), as long as the reader is actively engaging with the work rather than letting it float harmlessly by.

Chapter Four

Life with Elizabeth Barrett Browning, 1845–1861

So far we have been following Browning's artistic development more or less chronologically, without dealing with the events in his life. The reason, as I have said, is that nothing much happened in his private life during this period. For the first 33 years of his existence, Browning lived with his parents, affluent enough not to need to take up a career and able to devote himself to his poetry. On occasion he traveled abroad—to Russia, to Italy—but in general little happened to interfere with the placid tenor of life (except for his having to read some rather severe reviews). In 1845 this changed. The advent of Elizabeth Barrett in Browning's life was to mean a complete upheaval: he left not just his parental home, but his native country, embarking not just on a relationship, but upon one of the most famous love affairs of the century—and one of the most significant poetic pairings to boot.

The love affair with Elizabeth Barrett had a direct effect on Browning's verse. The fact that much of his writing during the time of his courtship and marriage explored the possibilities of love poetry is no coincidence. The courtship period itself survives in textual form, in the shape of the hundreds of love letters the couple exchanged. This correspondence is as rich and satisfying a text as any of Browning's works, and it has the added advantage (for critics) of illuminating Browning's creative process during the period 1845–1846. Usefully for us, Browning valued Elizabeth Barrett as a poet, considering her a much greater writer than himself (a view few have shared since, although Elizabeth Barrett's work is currently being reappraised by critics). He showed her much of his work in progress; she commented; and the comments more often than not became incorporated into the final draft. Many of the monologues to appear in *Dramatic Romances and Lyrics* (1845)—and some of Browning's later dramatic writing—are discussed in the letters.

I. Elizabeth Barrett

Elizabeth Barrett was born in 1806, making her Browning's senior by six years; by 1845 she was probably the most famous female poet in England. She grew up a delicate but passionate child in the Hereford-shire countryside at a house called (prophetically, perhaps) Hope End. Her parents, especially her father, doted on her, and both encouraged her early poetic writings. And the writings came thick and fast, with a fluency founded on a wide reading of the classics and a well-tuned ear. "Literature," she wrote at the age of 14 (rather precociously referring to her development in the past tense)—"Literature was the star which in future prospect illuminated my future days—it was the spur which prompted me . . . the aim . . . the very seal of my being. I was deter-mined . . . to gain the very pinnacle of excellence."[1] In her 15th year, she suffered the first attack of a mysterious but serious illness that was later to confine her entirely to her bed.

The death of Mrs. Barrett in 1828 was a severe blow to Elizabeth and her father. Then foreclosure on the mortgage of Hope End (Mr. Barrett was in financial difficulties) compelled the family to move, by 1835, to a much smaller house in central London. By this time, she had published, anonymously, three volumes of poetry—*The Battle of Marathon* (1820), *An Essay on Mind* (1826), and a translation of *Prometheus Bound* with other poems (1833). In 1838 her health worsened, and a burst blood vessel in her chest necessitated a lengthy period of rest by the seaside. While convalescing, she went through a series of tragedies. The young surgeon who had been attending her (and with whom it seems certain Elizabeth was in love) died suddenly in 1839. In 1840, her brother Sam died in Jamaica, and in the same year her favorite brother, Edward, drowned off the coast of Torquay.

From 1841 to 1846 Elizabeth Barrett lived the life of an invalid, con-fined in an upper bedroom in 50 Wimpole Street, London. Her father had become fiercely protective of her. Now she had nothing to do, was almost never allowed out. She continued writing, and her work began to be very well received, both by critics and the larger reading public: *The Seraphim, and Other Poems* (1838) was well reviewed, and her collection of 1844, *Poems*, made such an impact that her name was being seriously discussed as a possible future poet laureate. But her home life, if not exactly miserable, was certainly restrictive.

The most famous aspect of her father's overprotectiveness was his insistence that no suitor was worthy of her hand, a deep-rooted if unacknowledged desire on his part never to let his daughter out of his sight. This "tyranny" (as it has been frequently termed) was not reserved for Elizabeth only; all Mr. Barrett's adult offspring were treated as children and forbidden to marry. But it certainly meant that Elizabeth Barrett's room was the least likely place in London for a romance to flower and bear fruit.

A mutual friend suggested that Browning contact Elizabeth Barrett, as one poet to another, in late 1844. Consequently, on January 10, 1845, he wrote her the first of what was to become a long series of letters. He had never met her, but he had read her verse with enthusiasm. Indeed, a passage in her "Lady Geraldine's Courtship" (1844) must have struck him as very agreeable indeed, in the face of the general incomprehension and hostility with which ordinary critics greeted his work:

A modern volume,—Wordworth's solemn-thoughtful idyll,
Howitt's ballad-verse, or Tennyson's enchanted reverie,—
Or from Browning some "Pomegranate," which, if cut deep down the
      middle,
Shows a heart within blood-tinctured, of a veined humanity.
      (161–164)

Browning's first letter is striking for its sheer enthusiasm—in terms of Victorian propriety as much as in the context of a first letter to a complete stranger:

> I love your verses with all my heart, dear Miss Barrett—and this is no off-hand complimentary letter that I shall write . . . into me it has gone, and part of me has it become, this great living poetry of yours . . . I do, as I say, love these books with all my heart—and I love you too. (qtd. in Kintner, 1)

The startling admission "I love you" came before Browning had even met Elizabeth Barrett. She replied with decorum, and an equally hasty proposal of marriage on Browning's part was met with similar vigor: "You have said some intemperate things . . . fancies—which you will not say over again . . . but *forget at once*, . . . And this you will do *for my sake* who am your friend (and you have none truer)—and this I ask, because it is a condition necessary to our future liberty of intercourse" (qtd. in Kintner, 72–73). Approaching 40 and unwell, Elizabeth Barrett had good reason for caution: her fear (expressed in various ways in the letters) was that Browning's feelings were based on an idealized view of the poet rather than on the frail human reality. It certainly seems that Browning had decided he was going to fall in love with Elizabeth Barrett before he even knew her and that a tendency to idealize the poetic spirit was behind this decision. It hardly seems a sound basis for a relationship, particularly when we consider the withering atmosphere of parental disapproval that prevailed in 50 Wimpole Street. But what Elizabeth Barrett did not know was the sheer power with which Browning's imagination was able to transform idealization into emotional reality, to make it into a part of his mental furniture.

During the two years that followed, the two poets exchanged letters, often every day (and sometimes several times a day), and met regularly. What Browning had started impetuously he continued with diligence and application. They decided to restart their relationship not on Browning's sudden "I love you" but on a cooler note of friendship. They wrote of their everyday lives; they exchanged thoughts on poetry; they commented on each other's writing. Gradually their friendship ripened into love, and from there into thoughts of marriage. On September 12, 1846, Elizabeth Barrett secretly left Wimpole Street to join Browning at a nearby chapel to be married. After the ceremony, she returned to her father's house for a week, but then the two of them left England for Italy. They traveled first to Pisa and then in 1847 to Florence, where they settled in a house named "Casa Guidi." As they expected, Elizabeth's father was outraged; he immediately disinherited his daughter, and her name was not mentioned at 50 Wimpole Street again.

As marriages go, Browning and Elizabeth Barrett had a happy one. In Italy, Elizabeth Barrett discovered she was not such an invalid after all, and although she was never exactly hale, she traveled around Europe, gave birth to a son (after two miscarriages), and lived a full life. The cornerstone of their relationship was Browning's immense respect for women, Elizabeth Barrett in particular.

II. Browning and Women

Browning has a reputation as one of the great writers of heterosexual love poetry, yet an examination of Browning's representations of women reveals many difficulties. Most of these are contextual: the nineteenth century has a poor reputation when it comes to views of women. Victorian women had no vote, had limited rights to own property, had little access to education, and were in most important senses forced to depend upon men. The effective subordination of women was mirrored by an ideological figuring of them as superior moral beings, as pure and spiritual rather than rational entities (queens, angels in the house), that was in itself repressive.

We need to be careful here: no culture is so monolithic that it presents a single view on a subject so wide-ranging as "the rights of women." It is true, of course, that many prominent Victorian men regarded women as effectively children, and the burden of legislation was certainly straightforwardly repressive. John Ruskin, the widely respected writer and critic, gave voice in *Of Queen's Gardens* to a belief that women were simply inferior to men and that society ought to reflect that fact. Coventry Patmore's widely read poem of marriage, "The Angel in the House," articulated a vision of domestic happiness predicated on this view.

The phrase "the angel in the house" has been widely canvassed by critics as an encapsulation of this repressive ideology. The sense is that since woman is an angel, a madonna on a pedestal, it is simply inappropriate for her to partake in the messy real world. Thus, spared the opportunity of an education or earning a living for herself, she is to sit by the fire and darn while providing her husband with an emotional and moral center for his life. It should be pointed out, however, that Patmore's phrase has been equally widely misunderstood: "the angel in the house" is not a description of the wife in his marriage poem but an externalization of the love that exists between husband and wife. As soon as we posit a situation where women were repressed by a governing ideology, we start discovering important figures who contradict that very ideology. John Stuart Mill, the same man to have annotated Browning's *Pauline* so influentially, campaigned tirelessly for the emancipation of women, trying in the 1860s to pass legislation through Parliament giving them the vote. His *On the Subjection of Women* (1869) remains a very readable statement of basic feminism. In other words, Victorian England represents a transitional period in the movement toward modern-day feminism.

Browning displayed a distinct tendency to idealize women, and his literary representations of the female take shape from his own uxuriousness. He wrote to Elizabeth Barrett explaining that his love for her was rooted in a deeply felt sense of her superiority. There had been other women, but he had been unable to love them because

there must be this disproportionateness in a beloved object—before I
knew you, women seemed not much better than myself,—therefore, no
love for them! There is no love but from beneath, far beneath. (August
10, 1846; qtd. in Kintner, 950)

Elizabeth was understandably alarmed by the implications of this statement. "But when you say," she replied, "that there can be no love except
'from beneath' . . . is it right? Is it comforting to hear of? No, no—
indeed" (August 10, 1846; qtd. in Kintner, 953). But Browning was
adamant. "Do you not see how with this feeling," he wrote to her, "—
how much my happiness would be disturbed by allying myself with a
woman to whose intellect, as well as goodness, I could *not* look up?" He
adds that it is not just a question of admiring intellect and goodness, but
also of obeying—"in an obedience to whose desires, therefore, I should
not be justified in indulging?" (August 13, 1846; qtd. in Kintner, 960).
    This stance of the obedient devotee before the lofty female figure is
often elaborated in the poetry. In a poem which was very much the
product of the courtship years with Elizabeth Barrett, "The Flight of the
Duchess," the narrator saddles a horse for the Duchess's escape and
meditates on his own inferiority—"so far beneath her" that

> [I] would have been only too glad for her service
> To dance on hot ploughshares like a Turk dervise,
> But, unable to pay proper duty where owing it,
> Was reduced to that pitiful method of showing it.
>   (750–753)

The flipside of this reiterated sense of veneration of women in the early
work is darker and less defensible. The fate of many of the women in
Browning's early work is grisly. The female protagonists in "Porphyria's
Lover" and "My Last Duchess" are both violently murdered—by men
who link female sexuality and violence against women directly in their
minds. It is possible to trace a strand in Browning's work that leads up
to Pompilia in *The Ring and the Book*—his most complete elaboration of
female passivity and childishness, another heroine who is violently
murdered.
    It might be possible to construct a defence of the implied misogyny
of having so many women violently murdered by suggesting that
Browning is ironically commenting upon the tendency of men to dominate women. The Duke in "My Last Duchess," for instance, can be seen

as a satire upon the male desire to completely dominate and possess womanhood. More realistically, I think, we must read Browning's early representations of woman as derived from literature rather than real life; the tendency to see woman as either excessively pure or excessively wicked is a long-standing literary tradition (however unfortunate). Browning's marriage and increasing maturity necessarily distanced him from this tradition, if only to certain degree.

"The Flight of the Duchess" is a poem in which his increasing maturity can be seen. As with the earlier "My Last Duchess," Browning's starting point is a submissive woman in a repressive relationship with a powerful man, the same situation he found in the relationship between Elizabeth Barrett and her father in 50 Wimpole Street, although the first 215 lines of this poem had been written before Browning ever met her (they were published in *Hood's Magazine*, April 1845). The remainder of the poem was written and given to Elizabeth Barrett to comment upon. Browning approved of the suggestions she made: "For the criticism itself, it is all true, except the overrating—all the suggestions are to be adopted, the improvements accepted" (July 25, 1845; qtd. in Kintner, 135). In other words, the poem as we have it is made up of two parts written at different times.

The first, pre-EBB section, delineates the oppressive situation the Lady finds herself, the tyrannical temper of the Duke:

> So the little Lady grew silent and thin,
>   Paling and ever paling,
> As the way is with a hid chagrin;
>   And the Duke perceived that she was ailing,
> And said in his heart, " 'Tis done to spite me,
> But I shall find it in my power to right me!"
> Don't swear, friend—the Old One, many a year,
> Is in Hell, and the Duke's self . . . you shall hear. (208–215)

This is how the poem ended when first published in *Hood's Magazine*.

For months Browning let it lie before taking it up again with an image that had struck him on a holiday in Wales:

> Well, early in autumn, at first winter-warning,
> When the stag had to break with his foot, of a morning,

> A drinking-hole out of the fresh tender ice
> That covered the pond till the sun, in a trice,
> Loosening it, let out a ripple of gold,
> And another, and another, and faster and faster,
> Till, dimpling to blindness, the wide water rolled:
> Then it so chanced that the Duke out master
> . . . resolv[ed] on a hunting-party. (216–227)

The use here of an extended simile might be objected to as clogging the narrative. But, in fact, the beauty of "The Flight of the Duchess" resides precisely in moments such as this. The description of the stag breaking the ice functions as a subtle and beautifully appropriate image for the awakening of the Duchess herself. The Duke is hunting stags; his wife is like the stag, his victim; but like a stag she is tentatively unfreezing her own life. The Duke goes hunting while the Duchess stays behind. During the Duke's absence, an old Gypsy woman visits the Duchess, and the Duchess departs to begin a new life of freedom with the Gypsies.

The narrator of this poem is an aged servant, a man who automatically adopts the posture of subservience I have been talking about. But despite the male perspective, the Duchess's rebirth is presented in wholly female terms. The old Gypsy woman sits in the Lady's room "coiled at her feet like a child at ease, / The lady sat between her knees" (24–25). The notion of rebirth is emphasized by the location of the duchess, newborn between the Gypsy's legs. The Gypsy is singing a song ("mystic measure"), but the Duchess's rebirth seems to depend as much upon her eyes as her ears:

> For it was life her eyes were drinking
> From the crone's wide pair above unblinking,
> —Life's pure fire received without shrinking
> Into the heart and breast whose heaving
> Told you no single drop they were leaving. (540–544)

The whole scenario is feminized, from the mother-daughter dynamic between this queen of the Gypsies and the Duchess down to the feminine line endings that give the verse its onward fluidity. "Word took word as hand takes hand," says the narrator (563), and we are again reminded of Robert and Elizabeth's courtship, where words (spoken and written) took the place of the more conventional wooing based on human contact.

The narrator then relates some of the Gypsy's song, with its connective, loving burden ["love is the only good in the world. / Henceforth be loved as heart can love, / Or brain devise, or hand approve!" (615–617)], until something remarkable happens. The Gypsy's song is reaching a climax, with imagery that recalls the stag's dawn-breaking of the ice—

> "And then as, mid the dark, a gleam
>   "Of yet another morning breaks,
> "And like the hand which ends a dream,
> "Death, with the might of his sunbeam
>   "Touches the flesh and the soul awakes,
> "Then—"
>   Ay, then indeed something would happen!
> But what? For here her voice changed like a bird's;
> There grew more of the music and less of the words.
>   (684–691)

At this climactic, epiphanic moment, the narrator suddenly finds himself excluded. The talk, from one woman to another, passes beyond his ken, although he says that had the female servant Jacynth been there "to clap pen / To paper" then we might have a record of what passed. Browning is suggesting that this miraculous life-giving song is beyond the ability of a man to comprehend, although a woman would be able so to do. With the Duchess subsequently escaping in the company of the Gypsy, the picture that results is of women gaining strength from women, to the exclusion of men. The Duchess finally runs away from the tyrannical Duke in the company of the Gypsy woman, to start a new life.

This tale of a woman escaping the tyranny of a man (inspired as she is by the power of a queen) is profoundly unpatriarchal. Far from placing women on an ethereal pedestal in order to better control and dominate them, Browning seems to be genuinely writing himself out of the equation. The women in his poetry may be venerated, but they are also active, powerful, and (particularly after his meeting with Elizabeth Barrett) in control.

III. Married life, 1846–1855

1846 marked a complete upheaval for Browning. His previous life had been sedentary; living at home and having a closely knit group of family and friends, he had worked only at his poetry. After the marriage he went to live in a strange country at a time of intense political turmoil. Italy was in the process of affirming nationhood, fighting foreign occupation in the shape of Austrian troops. This cause of "Italian liberty" was taken up enthusiastically by both the Brownings; it became a theme in their poetry, particularly in hers. Indeed, the years 1846–1855 saw a great deal of poetry from the pen of Elizabeth Barrett Browning and a virtual silence from that of her husband. Elizabeth Barrett recorded her own perspective on the courtship and marriage in her sonnet sequence, *Sonnets from the Portuguese*, a title meant to disguise the intensely personal nature of the poetry. These 50 sonnets appeared in her collected edition of 1850, *Poems*, and in 1851 she published a collection celebrating the cause of Italian liberty (and lamenting the apparent collapse of those ideals). *Casa Guidi Windows* took its title from the marital home. Much of the rest of the 1850s was taken up with work on her largest poetic enterprise, the verse-novel *Aurora Leigh* (1857).

By contrast, Browning wrote practically nothing. His single publication during this near-decade was *Christmas-Eve and Easter Day* (1850), a poem that critics have traditionally seen as bearing the heavy impress of his wife's influence. As its title suggests, it is a poem on religious themes. In fact, this is the only poem in Browning's canon to directly address religious issues, and its dry, rather abstract style of discussion (particularly in the second part) is rather off-putting. In 1845, Elizabeth Barrett had asserted that contemporary poetry ought not to attempt to employ classical mythology as a subject because for any modern person the important questions relate to Christianity: "Christianity is a worthy *myth*, & poetically acceptable" (qtd. in Kintner, 43). She also encouraged Browning to write in his own voice, as she did—to aim at subjective poetry rather than objective poetry, as he had done hitherto.

The mode of "Christmas-Eve," the first of these two interconnected pieces, is almost grotesque in its levity and its fondness for bizarre rhymes ("garlic" "starlike," "affirm any" "Germany," "Manchester" "haunches stir," and so on). The speaker describes a visit to a nonconformist chapel to hear a sermon preached on Christmas Eve. Actually, he only goes into the chapel to get out of the rain, and he is not impressed by what he finds there. He is struck by "the preaching man's immense stupidity" (144) and the ugliness of the congregation ("the fat weary woman . . . the many-tattered / Little old-faced peaking sister-turned-mother . . . a tall yellow man, like the Penitent Thief" [48–81]). But on leaving the chapel in disgust, he has a startling vision:

> All at once I looked up with terror.
> He was there.
> He himself with his human air.
> On the narrow pathway, just before.
> I saw the back of him, no more—
> He had left the chapel, then, as I. (430–435)

This unnamed figure (we assume it is Christ) takes the narrator on a journey through the air, first to go to Mass in St. Peter's, Rome, and then to hear a lecture in Göttingen, Germany, on the new scientific methods of interpreting Christianity that were known as the Higher Criticism. At the end, awaking on the dingy benches of the chapel, the narrator seems to have learned the lesson that religious truth is relative (which is to say, no one has a monopoly) and that it is profoundly difficult to express—that the preacher should not be mocked because he fails at "making the square to a finite eye / The circle of infinity" (1270–1271). The vocabulary of finitude/infinitude should alert us to the fact that Browning is talking of more than religion, narrowly conceived. In fact, the narrator's insistence that his "Vision" of Rome and Göttingen really happened ("For the Vision, that was true, I wist, / True as that heaven and earth exist" [1244–1245])—when appearances suggest that it was nothing but a dream—this insistence raises all manner of questions about truth and falsehood, religious and otherwise.

"Easter Day," the second poem in the pairing, is rather more dry. The key phrase comes at the beginning: "How very hard it is to be / A Christian!" (1–2). Browning goes on to elaborate a dialogue wherein one speaker argues from the perspective of "faith" and another on grounds of "skepticism." We are again treated to a vision, this time (apparently) of the end of the world, and the poem ends by affirming the love of God. Neither "Christmas-Eve" nor "Easter Day" deserves a place in the pantheon of Browning's greatest achievements. Indeed, they marked something of a backward step into the experimental period; the bizarre versification and the attempt to write in his own voice did not work well.

Contemporary critics treated this publication respectfully, although without enthusiasm. It did nothing to enhance Browning's low reputation (selling a mere 200 copies). Meanwhile, Elizabeth Barrett was being openly canvassed for the position of poet laureate after Wordsworth's death in 1850. It is almost as if Browning had given up on his separate career as a poet, content instead to bask in the glory of his wife. The birth of his son and the death of his much-loved mother (both in 1849) may each, in separate ways, have discouraged him from working at poetry. The family visited Paris, returned to London, and found contentment in their Italian life. From the perspective of late 1850, it might have seemed that Browning's career was effectively over and that he was living through other poets. He read his wife's manuscripts carefully, advocating changes only cautiously, in the spirit of an inferior. In 1851 he wrote his essay on Shelley (the manuscript is dated "Paris, 4 December 1851").

But 1852 saw him change in temper. As a New Year's resolution, he promised himself to write a new poem every day throughout 1852. On the first of January he wrote "Love among the Ruins," on the second "Women and Roses," and on the third "Childe Roland to the Dark Tower Came." The resolution did not last longer, but it put Browning back into the habit of writing poetry, and he began assembling the 50 poems that were to appear in 1855 as his most famous collection, *Men and Women*.

Chapter Five

Men and Women, 1855

Browning's most famous and influential collection of poetry merits a chapter to itself, not only because of the individual excellencies of its poems but also because it represents the first completely successful synthesis of Browning's two poetic impulses, the subjective and the objective. Browning had written many short dramatic monologues for earlier collections, of course, but the poems of *Men and Women* mark a definite advance. The poems of *Dramatic Lyrics* and *Dramatic Romances and Lyrics* constitute, broadly speaking, two types. One has ties to traditional short narrative or lyric poetry and cannot really be called *dramatic monologue* ("Count Gismond," "In a Gondola," "The Pied Piper of Hamelin"). The other is the dramatic monologue in which the speaker has a view of the world that is distorted in some way—by, for instance, religious mania ("Johannes Agricola in Meditation"), greed ("The Bishop Orders his Tomb . . . "), hatred ("Soliloquy of the Spanish Cloister," "The Laboratory") or sheer insanity ("My Last Duchess," "Porphyria's Lover"). These monologues do indeed function as analyses of psychological conditions, but in a rather specialized way as representations of warped personalities. Though they combine objectivity and subjectivity, the subjectivity belongs wholly to the characters created and is taken to the extreme where it shades into madness. The objectivity, by the same token, is ours, the readers. We find ourselves judging the characters against our own perceptions of reality—characters such as the Duke in "My Last Duchess," who thinks it is acceptable to kill his wife if she does not live up to his impossible standards. We do not think so (at least, I hope we don't). It is the friction between these two positions that drives the poetry.

By the time he came to write *Men and Women*, however, Browning was creating characters of much greater subtlety and complexity. He no longer felt the need to mediate his monologues through personalities obviously insane or extreme—none of the poems in *Men and Women* take an insane perspective, with the possible exceptions of "Childe Roland to the Dark Tower Came" (significantly, an early work) and "Instans Tyrannus." The balance of objectivity and subjectivity is achieved via charac-

57

ters with whom it is much easier to empathize, characters derived from a wide range of historical periods but who nonetheless communicate on something approaching our own level.

In *Men and Women*, Browning drew together all his major concerns. His happy life with Elizabeth Barrett had produced a large body of poetry about love and marriage; his fascination with artistic and aesthetic questions had prompted the writing of many poems exploring the role of the artist. Of course, these two chief elements were linked by the fact that Browning and his wife were both artists and lovers, and it is this link that unifies an otherwise variegated collection.

I. "Grotesqueness": Form and Style

Men and Women was published in two volumes on November 10, 1855. As had been the case with several of his other publications, Browning seems to have expected it to become a popular success. He had written to a friend that he was "writing a sort of first step towards popularity," and he promised his publisher that his new volume would be "something saleable."[1] As had also been the case, he was disappointed in his hopes. Reviewers were not as scathing this time around, but they did describe what they saw as serious faults in Browning's conception of poetry. Although he claimed (in a letter to Edward Chapman, his publisher) to have "stopped [his] ears" against the reviewers, Browning was clearly stung by the response: "'Whoo-oo-oo-oo' mouths the big monkey—'Whee-ee-ee-ee' squeaks the little monkey and such a dig with the end of my umbrella as I should give the brutes if I couldn't keep my temper."[2]

Many reviewers objected to the subjects Browning chose to write about, but even more were hostile toward his distinctive style, and this is the criticism that has most dogged his reputation. The chief complaint had to do with "obscurity." At one end of the scale, George Eliot (in the *Westminster Review*, January 1856) talked of "a majestic obscurity which repels the ignorant"; at the other, the *Spectator* complained that the writing was likely "to baffle ordinary penetration." Writing later in the century, the critic Walter Bagehot distinguished between three poetic styles, modeled after three notable poets. The first he called the "Pure style," represented by Wordsworth; the second the "Ornate style," represented by Tennyson; and last and least is the style Bagehot christened "Grotesque," represented by Browning.

Wordsworth (Bagehot argues) speaks plainly, directly, and lucidly, which makes his poetry of the best sort. Tennyson cannot resist the occasional poetic flourish, the odd elaborate simile or strained image, but essentially Tennyson too is writing to be understood. But Browning's style is deliberately difficult, awkward, and ugly. Bagehot, of course, was exaggerating to make his point, but the fact remains even today that any critic of Browning's verse has to come to terms with his "grotesque" style.

Browning's difficult syntax and awkwardness of expression mirrors the awkwardness and difficulty inherent in comprehending experience. As a noted modern scholar puts it, Browning "thinks of matter, in whatever form, as something dense, heavy, rough, and strong flavored . . . it is by imitation of the roughness of a thing that one has most chance to get inside it. Things are not made of smooth appearances, but of the dense inner core which is best approached through heavy language":

> Grotesque metaphors, ugly words heavy with consonants, stuttering alliteration, strong active verbs, breathless rhythms, onomatopoeia, images of rank smells, rough textures, and of things fleshy, viscous, sticky, nubbly, slimy, shaggy, sharp, crawling, thorny, or prickly—all these work together in Browning's verse to create an effect of unparalleled thickness, harshness, and roughness . . . They are the chief means by which he expresses his sense of what reality is like.[3]

Browning is certainly capable of melodious, lyrical sweetness (as demonstrated by poems such as "Love among the Ruins" or "A Woman's Last Word"), but one of the distinguishing features of his dramatic monologues is this stylistic attempt to reproduce speech in all its stumblings and infelicities. His speakers often seem to grope for the right word.

> Who am I?
> Why, one, sir, who is lodging with a friend
> Three streets off—he's a certain . . . how d'ye call?
> Master—a . . . Cosimo of the Medici . . .
> ("Fra Lippo Lippi" [14–17])

He pays great attention to the pauses, stops, and lacunae of ordinary speech, using punctuation to underline the delivery.

> Just when I seemed about to learn!
>   Where is the thread now? Off again!
> The old trick! Only I discern—
>   Infinite passion, and the pain
> Of finite hearts that yearn.
>   ("Two in the Campagna" [56–60])

Browning's fascination with the sound of poetry often manifests itself in onomatopoeia:

> *Bang-whang-whang* goes the drum, *tootle-le-tootle* the fife;
> No keeping one's haunches still: it's the greatest pleasure in life.
>   ("Up at a Villa—Down in the City" [53–54])

> And nip each softling of a wee white mouse,
> *Weke, weke*, that's crept to keep him company!
>   ("Fra Lippo Lippi" [10–11])

The poetry is also full of exclamations and interjections: "G-r-r- you swine!" ("Soliloquy of the Spanish Cloister"); "Zooks . . . Boh!" ("Fra Lippo Lippi"); "Faugh! . . . ugh!" ("Childe Roland . . . ").

> Fee, faw, fum! bubble and squeak!
> Blessedest Thursday's the fat of the week.
> Rumble and tumble, sleek and rough,
> Stinking and savoury, smug and gruff.
>   ("Holy Cross Day" [1–4])

Browning's use of metaphor and his choice of imagery is often striking in the same way. The nightmarish landscape perceived by the knight in "Childe Roland to the Dark Tower Came" is realized in language arresting and horrible:

> As for the grass, it grew as scant as hair
>   In leprosy; thin dry blades pricked the mud
>   Which underneath looked kneaded up with blood.
> One stiff blind horse, his every bone a-stare,

Stood stupefied however he came there:
Thrust out past service from the devil's stud! (73–78)

The point here is not "grotesqueness" for the sake of it. The landscape that the narrator travels through is available to us only through the perceptions of the narrator himself—which, of course, is the whole point of the dramatic monologue. So this description tells us as much—if not more—about the mind of the narrator as it does about the land itself. Everything he sees is transformed by his overactive and paranoid imagination: "A sudden little river crossed my path / As unexpected as a serpent" (109–110); "It may have been a water-rat I speared, / But, ugh! it sounded like a baby's shriek" (125–126); "Then came some palsied oak, a cleft in him / Like a distorted mouth that splits its rim / Gaping at death" (154–156). By the close of the poem even the surrounding hills have taken on living characteristics:

The hills, like giants at a hunting, lay,
Chin upon hand, to see the game at bay,—
"Now stab and end the creature—" (190–192)

The effect, then, of the "grotesque" style and imagery (in this case, at any rate) is to link form and content, to accurately reproduce the contours of a paranoid imagination.

All these things add up to a poetic style that is often dense, clotted, and difficult; but for Browning difficulty was a necessary part of poetry. Much of his poetry can be initially puzzling, but sense usually reveals itself with the reader's perseverance. The poem "Popularity," for instance, deals with public ignorance and neglect of poetic genius, using John Keats as an example. But Browning's own experience as a poet, his failure (by 1855) to achieve popularity and his reputation as "obscure" is probably behind the stylistic complexity of the final lines of the poem:

XI

Mere conchs! not fit for warp or woof!
Till cunning come to pound and squeeze
And clarify,—refine to proof
The liquor filtered by degrees,
While the world stands aloof.

XII

And there's the extract, flasked and fine,
  And priced and saleable at last!
And Hobbs, Nobbs, Stokes and Nokes combine
  To paint the future from the past,
Put blue into their line.

XIII

Hobbs hints blue,—straight he turtle eats:
  Nobbs prints blue—claret crowns his cup:
Nokes outdares Stokes in azure feats,—
  Both gorge. Who fished the murex up?
What porridge had John Keats? (51–65)

This is a heavily compacted language; it is by analyzing such a passage that we can approach Browning's conception of poetic discourse. To understand the last stanza, for instance, involves us in determining what the strange-sounding word *murex* means (it is a type of shellfish from which is extracted a deep-blue colored dye—by extension, the coloring of this "royal" blue is used as a metaphor for poetic authenticity). We have to understand that the unexplained individuals "Hobbs, Nobbs, Stokes and Nokes" are lesser poets, who produce art only by imitating greater artists. A prose paraphrase of the final stanza might run as follows: Hobbs's art utilizes the "blue" of true art, and he is rewarded with luscious food; Nobbs does the same, and is rewarded with fine wines. Nokes and Stokes compete to produce the "bluest" poetry, and both enjoy popularity. But in all this we are likely to forget who it was who *first* produced this brilliant blueness—Keats. *He* was ignored in his own time, having to make do with mere "porridge." But in order to arrive at this understanding of the lines, we have to *work* at the poetry. Browning's poetry engages its readers; we have to play a part in constructing the sense, otherwise it is likely to pass us by.

Eight of the 50 poems in *Men and Women* are blank-verse dramatic monologues that elaborate on aesthetic and religious theories ("Fra Lippo Lippi," "Andrea del Sarto," "How It Strikes a Contemporary," "Transcendentalism," "An Epistle . . . of Karshish," "Bishop Blougrams Apology," "Protus," "Cleon"). The connection between art and religion was a central concern for Browning, God being (as he had said in

Paracelsus) "the perfect poet." The rest of the poems in the collection can be seen as stanzaic or rhymed dramatic monologues—the form that makes up the bulk of Browning's body of dramatic monologues, although you might be forgiven for thinking otherwise. It is interesting that Browning turned away from the more conscious artifice of rhyme and stanza when writing about the artifice of art. It is as if he needed the least cluttered format in order to discuss the nature of the beast, as if he felt freer to experiment with form when dealing with other matters.

II. The Blank-Verse Monologues: Poems about Artists

Browning turned to the visual arts as exempla of his aesthetic theories. In "Old Pictures in Florence," the speaker contrasts the perfection of eternity (in which the Old Masters dwell) with the necessary imperfection and finitude of life:

> They are perfect—how else? they shall never change:
> We are faulty—why not? we have time in store.
> The Artificer's hand is not arrested
> With us; we are rough-hewn, nowise polished. (123–126)

The speaker contrasts the alleged "perfection" of Greek art with the less polished productions of the Italian Renaissance, to point out that the latter are, paradoxically, better art. It is this apparent paradox that is elaborated in the monologues "Fra Lippo Lippi" and "Andrea del Sarto," two of Browning's most famous poems.

Lippi and del Sarto were both fifteenth-century Italian painters, and the speeches Browning puts into their mouths constitute his most direct explorations of the relationship between life and art. Lippi's monologue is full of spice and verve; he is a monk, but has very unmonkish tastes for fine food, wine, and women. On the orders of his superiors he paints religious subjects, but his real interest is in the curious and in human detail rather than in the pious subjects themselves. He believes in copying life in all its raggedness and roughness even though the prevailing artistic tenets of his age concerned the production of idealized, perfect images. The Prior criticizes Fra Lippo Lippi's realism (sounding as he does so like a typical Victorian critic attacking Browning's monologues):

"How, what's here?
Quite from the mark of painting, bless us all!
Faces, arms, legs and bodies like the true
As much as pea and pea! it's devil's-game!
Your business is not to catch men with show,
With homage to the perishable clay,
But lift them over it, ignore it all,
Make them forget there's such a thing as flesh." (175–182)

. But Lippi (and, by extension, Browning) cannot see his fascination with "the perishable clay" as a fault. His reasons for copying the world so exactly, warts and all, is an intensely religious one:

You be judge! . . .
. . . you've seen the world
—The beauty and the wonder and the power,
The shapes of things, their colours, lights and shades,
Changes, surprises,—and God made it all!
—For what? Do you feel thankful, ay or no,
For this fair town's face, yonder river's line,
The mountain round it and the sky above,
Much more the figures of man, woman, child,
These are the frame to? What's it all about?
To be passed over, despised? or dwelt upon,
Wondered at? oh, this last of course! (280–292)

Lippi insists that "this world's no blot for us, / Nor blank; it means intensely, and means good" (313–314). He is outlining an aesthetic that also expresses Browning's views, a defense of "grotesque art." Such a defense (for the visual arts) had also been proposed by Browning's friend the art critic John Ruskin. In his book on the Italian Renaissance, *The Stones of Venice* (1851–1853), he declared that

no good work whatever can be perfect, and *the demand for perfection is always a sign of misunderstanding of the ends of art*. This for two reasons, both based on everlasting laws. The first, that no great man ever stops working till he has reached his point of failure; that is to say, his mind is always far in advance of his powers of execution . . . The second reason is, that imperfection is . . . the sign of life in a mortal body, that is to say, of a state of progress and change. (II.6)

Browning's Andrea del Sarto represents the opposite extreme. Known as "the faultless painter" because of his perfect technique, del Sarto nonetheless feels that his work is actually a failure, and the nature of that failure is reflected in the grey, measured, and ultimately sterile tones of his monologue. It is too perfect, too cold and calm, to capture the essence of things. He considers that other, less polished artists have "a truer light of God in them" than he does (79) and gives us an example in one of Raphael's pictures: even though there seem to be things wrong with the draftsmanship ("The arm is wrongly put—and there again— / A fault to pardon in the drawing's lines" 111–112), nevertheless "its soul is right." Del Sarto understands the point and can frame it as a rhetorical question, but he cannot translate this understanding into his work:

> Ah, but a man's reach should exceed his grasp,
> Or what's a heaven for? All is silver-grey
> Placid and perfect with my art: the worse! (97–99)

There is more to these two wonderfully fertile poems than this bald summary of aesthetic philosophy suggests, of course. Lippo's creative powers are intimately connected with his sexuality—the occasion for the monologue is the fact that he has been caught in the doorway of a brothel. By way of explaining his errant sexual practices to the City Guard he slips naturally into elaborating his artistic theories, and he does this precisely because the two things are interconnected in his mind. Andrea del Sarto is also governed by a passion, and like Lippi it is a passion for a woman; the difference is that the woman is his wife. It is perhaps curious that Browning, in the middle of his own happy marriage, should have linked Andrea del Sarto's artistic failure to his uxuriousness. Perhaps Browning had suffered moments of doubt that in devoting himself too greatly to his wife he was damaging his art. Yet Elizabeth Barrett was a very different sort of person than Lucrezia, the wife in "Andrea del Sarto." She is beautiful and has served as model for her husband's paintings of the Virgin Mary, but she has also taken many lovers and is awaiting the arrival of some paramour while del Sarto addresses her. The connection seems to be that del Sarto is a failure as a

husband because he loves his wife too much, just as he is a failure as a
painter because his technique is too "flawless." But the missing quantity
is perhaps the most important thing in Browning's psychological equation: energy. Unlike the bawdy and passionate excuses of the sinful
monk in "Fra Lippo Lippi," the grey, Chekhovian tones of "Andrea del
Sarto" tend rather to alienate us from the speaker.

Without wishing to strain the point, it would be fair to say that
"energy" is the currency of Browning's work—the same energy and
urgency conveyed by the clipped, sometimes mangled textures of his style.
This is the reason why the speaker in "Soliloquy of the Spanish Cloister" is
so much more appealing as a character, for all his violent and irrational
hatred, than the more balanced but rather insipid Andrea del Sarto.

A similar moral is inculcated in "Transcendentalism: A Poem in
Twelve Books." Here the speaker upbraids the author of the musty-
sounding epic referred to by the title of the poem on the grounds that
his work, though written as poetry, is actually prose. The poet should be
inspired, passionate, a medium for energy. "You speak, that's your error.
Song's our art" (2). A poet should not "speak"; if it is speaking he is
interested in, "speak prose and hollo it till Europe hears!" (11). But
poetry "buries us with glory, young once more, / Pouring heaven into
this shut house of life" (44–45). Exuberance is more important than
precision, even if we read *exuberance* to mean "roughness" and *precision* to
mean "perfection." "The Grammarian's Funeral" makes a similar
point—the grammarian pedant in question having wasted his life on
dry inquiries, such as into "the doctrine of the enclitic *de*," while being
himself "dead from the waist down" (131–132). Similarly, the drily
mathematical music of "Master Hughes of Saxe-Gotha" is tedious for
the poor organist who has to play it; it "taxes the finger" without providing access to the golden "Truth."

In each of these poems Browning elaborates a "subjective" point—
the practice of art, something close to his own heart—with an "objectivity" that adds distance and definition to the undertaking. His artists—
painters, poets, musicians—are, almost without exception, misunderstood
by their contemporaries. Producing art true to their own principles, they
are rejected or ignored by their audience. Clearly, this is a state of affairs
that Browning knew intimately. We might almost call his poems about
art autobiographical—almost, but not quite. Because, of course, the
speakers of these poems both are and are not Browning.

The poet described in "How It Strikes a Contemporary," for instance,
is in a situation similar to Browning's. The public has certain set notions

about him—that he lives in incredible opulence, eats his supper "in a room / Blazing with lights, four Titians on the wall, / And twenty naked girls to change his plate!" (75–77). But the truth is very different, for this poet is a modest and relatively poor man. The point is that how it strikes a contemporary is unlikely to be the truth of the matter. A poet cannot but observe the world, and it is his or her duty to observe it as accurately as possible; but the world, as Browning had discovered to his cost, did not return the compliment.

The narrator of "A Toccata of Galuppi's" is a person listening to one of the musical compositions of this Venetian composer. There can be no doubting the effectiveness of this music (as opposed to the failings of Master Saxe-Gotha's); the speaker gives voice to the vividness of the Venetian scenes the music conjures up:

> Here you come with your old music, and here's all the good it brings.
> What, they lived once thus at Venice, where the merchants were the
>   kings,
> Where Saint Mark's is, where the Doges used to wed the sea with
>   rings?

> Ay, because the sea's the street there; and 'tis arched by . . . what you
>   call
> . . . Shylock's bridge with houses on it, where they kept the carnival:
> I was never out of England—it's as if I saw it all. (4–9)

This homebound speaker (clearly not Browning, who had been "out of England" for nearly ten years) might be disposed to praise a composer capable of such vivid powers of evocation. But the opposite is the case. In a sense, Galuppi's work is too evocative, too powerful, because it brings home to the speaker his own sense of mortality. He sees the people of bygone Venice as dead and gone, "merely born to bloom and drop . . . Dust and ashes" (40–44). The beautiful women who had graced the balls and dances at which Galuppi played are beautiful no longer:

> Dear dead women, with such hair too—what's become of all the gold
> Used to hang and brush their bosoms? I feel chilly and grown old.
>   (44–45)

Most critics have seen this complex poem as an implied criticism of the artist—a composer who, like Master Hughes of Saxe-Gotha, builds elaborately mathematical but ultimately empty constructions, works that leave the sense of "dust and ashes" in the listener's mind.[4] But surely this is not the case; the problem here is with the listener, not with Galuppi's music. There can be no doubt of the evocative power of a toccata that manages to imaginatively transport an Englishman who has never left his country over the sea and back through time—"it's as if I saw it all." The dessicating array of technical terms with which the poem is scattered—"lesser thirds," "sixths diminished," "suspensions," "commiserating sevenths," "the dominant's persistence"—belong to the analyzing mind of the (English) speaker, rather than the flowing music of Galuppi himself. In fact, the speaker is quite specific about why he dislikes Galuppi's music:

> But when I sit down to reason, think to take my stand nor swerve,
> While I triumph o'er a secret wrung from nature's close reserve,
> In you come with your cold music till I creep thro' every nerve.
>
> (31–33)

He is the epitome of English rationality, and he resents the power Galuppi's music has to move him. Once again, the theme is the inability of the audience to appreciate the work of the artist. The tendency of the narrator to express his vision in economic terms may also express Browning's frustration with the commercialism of 1850s Britain. Venice is the town "where the merchants were the kings" (5), "where the Doges used to wed the sea with rings" (6); the decline of the city is expressed as "Venice spent what Venice earned" (35)—even the hair of the beautiful women is "gold" (45). The triumph of monetary greed over love is articulated via a similar metaphor—the "golden" hair of a beautiful woman—in a poem from the later collection *Dramatis Personae*, "Gold Hair: A Story of Pornic."

III. Religious Questions and the Grotesque

Throughout the 1850s and 1860s, from *Christmas-Eve and Easter Day* onwards, Browning wrote poetry that investigated religious questions. As I have suggested, religion and poetry were for Browning interconnected entities. Browning's fascination with the visual arts, particularly painters, allowed him to examine from an interdisciplinary perspective a variety of aesthetic questions concerning his own poetry and the way it had been attacked by critics. In a number of poems with religious themes, Browning examines questions of truth and falsehood, interpretation, and the way we read and understand texts.

The off-puttingly titled "An Epistle Containing the Strange Medical Experience of Karshish, the Arab Physician" is as much a document of historical reconstruction as an examination of religious matters. Karshish is an Arab doctor—the name in English means "the gatherer" ("The picker-up of learning's crumbs" is how it is rendered in the poem's first line)—and one of the curious pieces of information he has come across in his travels is the story of Lazarus, who was raised from the dead. Karshish, as a non-Christian, attempts to make sense of this event, to rationalize it (he reasons that Lazarus must have been suffering from "epilepsy" [80] and assumes that Christ, "the Nazarene," was "a learned leech" [247] or physician, able to cure the disease). Karshish puts down as madness Lazarus's claim of having been raised from the dead by the Son of God; and though he is strangely attracted to the new religion ("The very God! think, Abib; dost thou think? . . . The madman saith He said so: it is strange" [304–312]), he remains the rationalist. Indeed, his secular epistle seems to exist as a skeptical, worldly equivalent to the sacred epistles we find in the New Testament. Even his name, "the gatherer," has Christian resonance (a shepherd is a gatherer, as is a fisherman, and both are Christian types). In other words, we can read Karshish's "Epistle" as a rationalist parallel to the epistles of the New Testament. In the Europe of the 1850s a number of scholars, of which G. F. Strauss is only the most famous example, were seeking to explain the Bible in rational, scientific terms; clearly Browning's poem has contemporary relevance. If we see dying as being "gathered" to God, which is a conventional way of looking at it, then "Karshish" contains some interesting ironies. Karshish is the gatherer, but Christ has un-gathered Lazarus, has prevented God's gathering of him.

"Cleon," like "Karshish," is in the form of a letter from the first century A.D. written by an outsider to Christianity who nonetheless has heard of some of the events detailed in the New Testament. Whereas Karshish is a scientist, Cleon is an artist, so in a sense we can take this poem alongside the other monologues of *Men and Women* in which artists are the narrators. But where Browning's other artists tend, in one way or another, to stand outside the artistic mainstream of their day, Cleon is a great success. He combines (on his own admission) the excellencies of

the greatest artists of the classical world—Homer, Terpander, Phidias—
and his audience applauds him; yet he is not happy. His correspondent,
the king Protus, wonders if his work "accepted so by men . . . ([his] soul
thus in men's hearts) / [He] must not be accounted to attain / The very
crown and proper end of life?" Protus argues that Cleon has achieved
immortality through his art, but (like Woody Allen) Cleon would rather
achieve it by not dying:

> my fate is deadlier still,
> In this, that every day my sense of joy
> Grows more acute, my soul (intensified
> By power and insight) more enlarged, more keen;
> While every day my hairs fall more and more,
> My hand shakes, and the heavy years increase—
> The horror quickening still from year to year,
> The consummation coming past escape. (309–316)

The consummation is death, and the thought that death is the end,
that there is no afterlife, paralyzes Cleon. Browning himself was not in
this predicament because his Christian faith told him there was an afterlife. As with *Karshish*, this non-Christian narrator has encountered
Christianity, for in a postscript to his letter Cleon promises to deliver one
of Protus's epistles to the figure we now know as St. Paul, "Paulus: we
have heard his fame" (340), although he is not certain whether Paul and
Christ are not actually one and the same person. But he cannot believe
that "a mere barbarian Jew . . . Hath access to a secret shut from us"
(343–345). Christianity itself is mentioned only in the last few lines of
the poem.

> certain slaves
> Who touched on this same isle, preached him and Christ;
> And (as I gathered from a bystander)
> Their doctrine could be held by no sane man. (350–353)

The irony, of course, is that from Browning's Christian, nineteenth-
century perspective, Cleon's lack of faith was not quite sane; this
apparently obscure religion had come to dominate half the globe,
while Cleon had fallen into total obscurity ("Cleon" is actually a fic-

tional character, but we get the point). Indeed, the Greek name "Cleon" means "Famous," and "Protus" ("First") is an appropriate name for a king; both appellations are nicely ironic. Just as ironic is the fact that, in the poem, the man who has actually become "famous" and "first" has a name that Cleon cannot even get right: "one called Paulus . . . Indeed, if Christus be not one with him." (340–341) (Cleon is confused because "Christus," meaning "anointed one," is a title rather than a name like "Paulus.") As with so many of Browning's poems, the "facts" depend upon the point of view, or in this case the historical perspective.

Browning's Christianity was of a liberal humanist sort that stressed the New Testament principles of love and forgiveness. "Saul," for instance, is about an Old Testament subject, but Browning treats it with so many instances of New Testament typology, including direct reference to the Messiah ("the Godhead! I seek and I find it. O Saul, it shall be / A Face like my face . . . See the Christ stand!" [309–312]), that it might as well be a New Testament poem. "Holy Cross Day" distances Browning from the antisemitic strand that had so often manifested itself in Christianity.

More complex is "Bishop Blougram's Apology," perhaps the greatest and certainly the subtlest religious poem from *Men and Women*. The title's "Apology" refers to a formal explication of one's position or actions, and the Bishop of the title is a Roman Catholic defending himself against charges of hypocrisy and timeserving to an agnostic journalist, Gigadibs. Blougram was modeled, as Browning later admitted, on Cardinal Wiseman, one of the leading English Catholic clergyman of the age. The charge of hypocrisy arises for Blougram, as it did for Wiseman, from the looseness of his beliefs. In effect, Gigadibs says to Blougram, "You don't really believe in Christianity at all! How can you go on as a Bishop under these circumstances? How can you suggest that your belief is any better than my non-belief?" Blougram's reply is to sidestep such a simplistic right-or-wrong argument. Blougram says that if "faith" must necessarily be "absolute and exclusive," "I do not believe" (161–163). This might be thought of as a difficult position for a Churchman to hold, and consequently Blougram's arguments have been condemned by some critics as "hypocritical" and "special pleading." But for all his faults it seems likely that Blougram's defence of a relativist position contains the germ of Browning's own position. As the narrator declares of Blougram, "he said true things, but called them by wrong names" (996).

That way [of Christian Faith]
Over the mountain, which who stands upon
Is apt to doubt if it be meant for a road;
While, if he views it from the waste itself,
Up goes the line there, plain from base to brow,
Not vague, mistakable! what's a break or two
Seen from the unbroken desert either side?
And then (to bring in fresh philosophy)
What if the breaks themselves should prove at last
The most consummate of contrivances
To train a man's eye, teach him what is faith?
And so we stumble at truth's very test!
All we have gained then by our unbelief
Is a life of doubt diversified by faith,
For one of faith diversified by doubt:
We called the chess-board white,—we call it black. (198–212)

Blougram seems to be arguing for a subtle dialectical sense of doubt and faith in place of the old black-and-white certainties, and such a position might seem especially pertinent in the carefully-thought-through uncertainties of deconstruction literary theory. But at the same time, the shift from "faith diversified by doubt" to "doubt diversified by faith" marks a distinct decline in belief, the same fact of nineteenth-century religious life that Arnold mournfully noted in "Dover Beach." What critics of this poem tend to miss, whether they are favorably inclined toward Blougram or not, is how a barely submerged form of self-hatred informs a great deal of what he says and does. His repeated insistence that Gigadibs hates him—"you despise me," "you do despise me," "contempt . . . it's yours!" (13, 50, 431)—despite protestations to the contrary ("nay, I beg you, sir!") suggests a motivation rooted in Blougram's own sense of his own inadequacies. His certainty that he will never be Pope (62), his often savage self-characterizations ("Grant I'm a beast, why, beasts must live beasts' lives" [349]), and the way he implicitly admits he lacks "self-delight" (500) lend the apology as a whole a rather desperate edge. In effect, Blougram is not so much trying to convince Gigadibs as himself. The apparently urbane, worldly-wise chatter of the Bishop emerges as a sort of defensive reflex, the patina of a figure aware of a considerable body of anti-Catholic prejudice in his home country. He imagines the reaction he will get when Gigadibs publishes the account of their conversation:

> Why, men as soon would throw it in my teeth
> As copy and quote the infamy chalked broad
> About me on the church-door opposite. (964–966)

Blougram uses his intimacy with Gigadibs to try to explain himself, but he seems sure that Gigadibs will go on "detesting" and "defaming" him (968–970). Browning's objectivity sees Blougram's "hypocrisy" as both a real failing and symptomatic of the Catholic church; but Browning's subjectivity cannot help but empathize with the Bishop, in particular with the love of luxury as an overreaction to his underdog situation in Britain. It is no coincidence that Blougram's dominant image or "simile" (99)—used throughout the poem to suggest the way a person should confront life and faith—is of a journey over the ocean, away from the restrictions of Britain and toward the religious toleration of the United States. It is also perhaps not surprising that Cardinal Wiseman, the leading Catholic of the day and the original of Blougram, thought the poem "in its way triumphant."

Despite Blougram's insistence that Gigadibs "detests" him, Gigadibs's actual reaction is more complex and ambiguous. At the poem's end we are told that he was so struck by his conversation with the Bishop that he went on a voyage of his own, to Australia, like the subject of Browning's earlier poem "Waring." There he has given up his journalist ambitions and bought "settlers implements." The poem concludes,

> there—I hope,
> By this time he has tested his first plough,
> And studied his last chapter of St. John. (1012–1014)

Critics have detected an ambiguity in the last line (does it mean that Gigadibs has given up the study of religion? Or taken it up, beginning with the last chapter of John's Gospel?). Yet it seems clear that "his last chapter" means something other than "*the* last chapter" and that Gigadibs is trying to live life as life and not through books. The significant detail is that Gigadibs has run away, escaped; and escapees in

Browning—such as "Waring," the Duchess in "The Flight of the Duchess," and Pompilia in *The Ring and the Book*—are semi-heroic figures, worthy of celebration. "Blougram" is a poem that celebrates the vigor of the escapee, even when, as with Bishop himself, that status makes him seem oddly insoucient about the grand pieties of organised religion.

Chapter Six

The 1860s. *Dramatis Personae*

I. Elizabeth Barrett Browning Dies

Browning spent the winter of 1856–1857 deeply depressed by the negative reception of *Men and Women*; he could not bring himself to write any more poetry. He had produced the best poetry he was capable of, and it had come to nothing. Dearly as he loved Elizabeth, matters cannot have been helped by the huge success of her modern-day epic, *Aurora Leigh*. Published in November 1856, it was immediately greeted by reviewers and general readers not just as immeasurably superior to anything that Browning himself had written, but by some (John Ruskin, for instance) as "the finest poem the nineteenth century has produced in any language."[1] The disparity between his own and his wife's reputation must have sorely puzzled Browning. Elizabeth was praised for writing an epic; his own attempt at epic, *Sordello*, had engendered abuse, disdain, even hilarity. Critics were particularly impressed by the way Elizabeth had been unafraid to tackle strong subjects in her poem—the "woman" question, the conflict between rich and poor, rape—yet Browning was excoriated as "dirty-minded" for discussing similar topics in his dramatic monologues.

Although artistically baffled, if only for a time, at least Browning's financial worries came to an end shortly after *Men and Women*. John Kenyon, a close friend and supporter of both Brownings, died after a long illness on December 3, 1856. Kenyon had been a wealthy man, and his will included a large number of bequests to artists and writers, including one to Robert (£6,500) and one to Elizabeth (£4,500). In the 1850s, when an English laborer could live on a salary of a few pounds a year and an Italian laborer make do on considerably less, £11,000 was a colossal sum. Browning never knew financial hardship again; not that he had exactly known financial hardship before, but the Kenyon bequest did at least enable him to do what he wished with his future.

In fact, the gift very nearly put paid to the remainder of Browning's career as a writer. With no need to work and depressed over his failure to make a name as a poet, Browning drifted for several years. He took up drawing, practiced music, studied theology, helped teach his son French, walked, traveled about Europe. But soon a larger issue was to occupy his attention. Elizabeth's health was steadily worsening. In June 1861 the couple planned a holiday in France, but instead Elizabeth caught a cold that swiftly advanced into inflammation of the lungs. Her breathing grew more and more difficult. In the early morning of June 29, she died in Browning's arms after telling him, "our lives are held by God."

Browning was, of course, grief-stricken; but the end was not unanticipated. After the funeral Browning took his son and left Florence, never to return to the city. He remained passionate about Italy, but Florence carried too many memories of Elizabeth. He insisted to the end of his days that "his heart was forever buried in the tomb with Elizabeth Barrett." But, at the same time, Elizabeth's death seemed to unfreeze Browning's own creativity. His letters from this time are full of elaborate, even over-elaborate, expressions of grief; he describes himself as "miserably imperfect now" and declares, "my root is taken, nothing remains." He wrote to a friend that staying in the house he had shared with his wife was almost unbearable: "I began to go to pieces." Yet, at the same time, he could write to another friend, "do not imagine I am prostrated with grief." "I want my life to resemble that last fifteen years as little as possible" he told the Storys. He transferred his wife's money to accounts in his own name and packed up his belongings to leave Casa Guidi forever. Whereas Elizabeth had always declared her passionate and undying love of Italy and all things Italian, Browning now could resolutely announce, "I am English," and assert that Elizabeth was also "pure English to the hatred of all un-English cowardice, vituperation and lies." Whereas Elizabeth had treated their son, Pen, like a doll, keeping his curly hair long and providing him with girlish dresses (Browning had never approved of this), Browning could now get the boy's hair cut and have him dressed in long trousers. He wrote to his sister that "the golden curls and fantastic dress are gone just as Ba is gone." Shortly afterwards, Browning left Italy for England.

Browning's attitude to his wife's death is rather contradictory. He seemed simultaneously desolated and relieved to be rid of her. When a friend offered him a position as editor of the literary magazine *The Cornhill*, Browning turned it down, saying, "my life [is] done for and settled"; but at the same time he was starting to write again with a fluency and energy he had not known for many years. He edited his wife's volume *Last Poems*, saw it through the press in 1862, and then prepared a group of her essays for publication under the title of *The Greek Christian*

Poets and the English Poets. But if these efforts might have suggested that he was prepared to give over his writing life to being his wife's literary executor, he also revised and published a collected edition of his own poems (in three volumes, 1863), work which included radically revising *Sordello* among other things. A selected edition, edited by two friends, was also published in 1863. The reception of these two editions was so good, and they sold so well, that Browning's publishers persuaded him to postpone his new volume of poetry for another year, for fear of clogging the market. Amazing as it may seem, the same Browning who could not win popularity and respect under any conditions while his wife was alive (or so it seemed) was becoming famous and best-selling almost immediately after her death, without even needing to produce new work. When *Dramatis Personae* did finally appear on May 28, 1864, it served to set the seal on Browning's newfound success. The turnaround in Browning's reputation had finally arrived. From here on until the day of his death, Browning became consistently more and more widely praised and lionized.

It is important, particularly for a proper sense of the remainder of Browning's poetic output, to try to understand his contradictory feelings concerning Elizabeth Barrett. It is difficult to doubt that Browning loved his wife deeply and that he was genuinely moved by her loss; but at the same time there was an element of subconscious relief in her going away, a sense that she had overshadowed and to a certain extent stifled him poetically. It is not that Browning was in any way glad that his wife was dead; but his attitude toward her memory was consistently marked by both a straightforward grief and a sense of guilt, of obscure abandonment and betrayal. Browning found himself acting out a dual role: on the one hand he publicly praised his wife and everything connected with her (and editing her posthumous publications); on the other hand he wrote and published poetry that specifically attacked things she had held dear, such as her belief in spiritualism (in "Mr Sludge"), her political affiliation (in *Prince Hohenstiel-Schwangau*), her entire aesthetic—the things she believed poetry ought to be (in *The Ring and the Book*).

Many of the poems in *Dramatis Personae* are concerned with bad marriages, the breakdown of relationships, infidelity and betrayal. "Wives" are important subjects in the later Browning—abandoned ("James Lee's Wife"), dead (in *Balaustion's Adventure*), or betrayed by an adulterous husband (in *Fifine at the Fair*). Browning's attitude toward his dead wife—toward women in general—was profoundly problematic. It was not a simple matter of venerating Elizabeth's memory, nor of thankfully putting her behind him. Browning experienced both of these contradictory impulses at once. It may have been this emotional and intellectual turmoil that provided the impetus for what was by far the most productive and fertile period of Browning's writing life: 1864–1880.

II. *Dramatis Personae* (1864)

The eighteen poems of *Dramatis Personae* seem at first glance to have a wide variety of different topics and themes: broken marriage ("James Lee's Wife"), perfect music ("Abt Vogler"), religious belief ("A Death in the Desert"), religious misbelief ("Caliban upon Setebos"), the honoring of the memory of Elizabeth Barrett (various poems), and the discrediting of one of her central beliefs ("Mr Sludge, 'The Medium'"). Yet one theme was coming to dominate Browning's writing: infidelity, a concept that has several layers of meaning. Marriage is a convenient vehicle for exploring this theme as the partners may be unfaithful to one another literally (adulterously), emotionally, or intellectually. Infidelity was also an appropriate topic in terms of Browning's fascination with interpretation: the extent to which we adequately read, interpret, and judge the written word, the extent to which we are faithful or even can be faithful to texts, exercises him considerably.

"James Lee's Wife," the first poem in the collection, addresses this theme straightforwardly. The story is of a couple newly married who genuinely love one another and yet who break up. They separate not despite their love for one another, but perversely because of it. Browning himself (in a letter to Julia Wedgwood dated December 25, 1864) summed up the work: "People newly married, trying to realize a dream of being sufficient to each other . . . and finding it break up—the man being *tired* at first,—and tired precisely of the love." It is easy to see a personal significance in the man's dilemma, although the poem itself is presented wholly from the point of view of the wife.

"James Lee's Wife" is made up of nine separate lyrics, each with a title that specifies the place from which the unnamed wife speaks the words of the lyric: "James Lee's Wife Speaks at the Window," "By the Fireside," "In the Doorway," "Along the Beach," "On the Cliff," "Reading a Book, under the Cliff," "Among the Rocks," "Beside the Drawing Board," and finally "On Deck" (of a ship that is carrying her away from her husband). Each lyric has a different meter, line length, and rhyme scheme; as with Tennyson's recently published *Maud* (1855), the effect is one of discontinuity, the different forms reproducing the dissonance and fragmentation of the narrator's experience. But whereas in *Maud* the fragmentation is that of the narrator's own sanity, in "James Lee's Wife" the fragmentation is that of the relationship between the narrator and her husband; pained by her husband's withdrawal, she still remains sure of her own love. Despite their disparateness, the lyrics do work together. There is the same sense of dialectic that we noticed in earlier monologues.

The lyrics themselves are mediated along a series of contrasts that express differences between the couple. The first two lyrics—" . . . at the Window" and "By the Fireside"—divide day and night between them. In " . . . at the Window" the wife, on one side of the window, sees her husband on the other side. Everything seems polarized in an absolute, black-and-white fashion. "The world has changed," she says, "Summer has stopped" (2–7), as if a season could suddenly stop and be replaced by another, instead of gradually altering. "By the Fireside" explores a series of sharply differentiated contrasts, beginning with the wood burning on the fire: it is "shipwreck wood" and leads the narrator to contemplate the drowned sailors that once sailed in the bark. She imagines them under the sea jealously watching their seaside home:

> A ruddy shaft our fire must shoot
>   O'er the sea:
> Do sailors eye the casement—mute,
>   Drenched and stark,
>   From their bark—
> And envy, gnash their teeth for hate
> O' the warm safe house and happy freight
>   —Thee and me? (30–37)

The contrasts are extreme: fire and water, dry land and the bottom of the sea, the safety of the house and the peril suffered by the sailors, and above all the opposition between love and hatred. The house (with its "freight") is likened to a ship, but the final line is ambiguous. It might be contrasting the divisive hate of the drowned sailors with the harmony of "thee and me"; or it might be instancing "thee and me" as opposite as fire and water, a house and a sunken ship. When the lyric ends with a further simile—"Love's voyage full-sail,—(now gnash your teeth!) /

When planks start, open hell beneath"—it becomes clear that the man
and the woman are binary opposites.

If " . . . at the Window" and "By the Fireside" contrast (respectively)
day and night, the next two lyrics—"In the Doorway" and "Along the
Beach"—contrast inside and outside. The first lyric establishes an opposition between the cold, uninviting winter landscape outside and the possibility of safety and security inside the house (and, by extension, inside the
marriage). But "Along the Beach" makes plain that the marriage will
provide no shelter. Appropriately, the metaphors change from ones of
house and home to ones of nature. Addressing the husband she says,

> Oh Love, Love, no, Love! not so, indeed!
>   You were just weak earth, I knew:
> With much in you waste, with many a weed,
> And plenty of passions run to seed. (97–100)

The man is imaged as a wasteland, and the wordplay balances idiom
with literalism (are we to read "run to seed" as metaphor or as literal?
both?). It seems that "light, light love" has "wings to fly / At suspicion
of a bond" (117–118). The next two lyrics contrast location: one is "up"
("On the Cliff") and the other "down" ("Reading a Book under the
Cliff"), up and down being both literal and figurative quantities. In the
former lyric the narrator is hopeful that love may yet settle on the ugli-
est of surfaces, like a butterfly on an old rock. In the latter, however, she
has become resigned to the end of her marriage. The book James Lee's
wife is reading, incidently, is by none other than Robert Browning; the
lyric begins by quoting the six stanzas of a poem originally published in
the *Monthly Repository* in 1836 ("Still ailing, wind? wilt be appeased or
no? . . . "). The wife reads the lines as symptomatic of nothing so much
as "young man's pride"—a young man without the experience to realize
how fully transient happiness is. "Nothing can be as it has been before,"
she observes. "Nothing endures: the wind moans saying so" (212, 222).
The next two lyrics, "Among the Rocks" and "Beside the Drawing
Board," contrast the natural and the artificial—a positive portrait of
"the brown old earth" setting "his bones / To bask i' the sun," on the one
hand, and a gloomier meditation involving the drawing of a cast of a
working girl's hands, on the other. By the time we reach the final lyric,
"On Deck," we realize the extent to which opposing forces (day/night,
land/sea, natural/artificial) make the whole of "James Lee's Wife" a deli-

cate balancing act that expresses the precarious balance between man and woman, between love and indifference. This in turn explains the poem's fascination with liminality, with the boundaries between different states: the doorway between inside and outside, the beach between land and sea.

"James Lee's Wife" is well chosen as the keynote poem for *Dramatis Personae*. The same sense of liminality, change and flux, and impermanence inhabits virtually all the poems in the collection. In "Gold Hair: A Story of Pornic," the beauty of the central character is so fine, so rarified, that "her parents said" it was meant "to just see earth, and hardly be seen, / And blossom in heaven instead" (8–10). And this beauty is indeed transient; the girl, with her white skin and glorious golden hair, dies, her last wish being that nobody disturb the golden hair: "let it stay in the grave . . . Leave my poor gold hair alone" (34–35). Her wishes are observed, and the lady acquires the reputation of a saint. But eventually, while the church is being repaired, it is discovered that the girl had hidden a quantity of real gold in her hair. The discovery that the beautiful girl had been a miser sadly disillusions the people of Pornic, the narrator of the poem apparently included, likening as he does the discovery to Judas's 30 pieces of silver, to "a spider found [in] the communion-cup":

> Gold! She hoarded and hugged it first,
> Longed for it, lean'd o'er it, loved it—alas—
> Till the humour grew to a head and burst. (107–109)

This image, in which the beautiful girl is compared to a boil, infected with miserliness, is revolting enough. But the point of the poem is surely to compare transience and permanence. As with "James Lee's Wife," there is a sense in which nothing can be seen as permanent, not even that proverbial untarnishable, gold. It is impermanent both in the sense that you can't take it with you when you die, however much you might like to, but also in the sense that any such obsession leads to corrosion of the soul. The poem is a testament to what it calls "The Corruption of Man's Heart" (150).

"The Worst of It" is also about a broken-down marriage, this time from the point of view of the man. Love is again proven transient rather than eternal, but the irony is that the man's constancy turns out to be a worse choice than the wife's inconstancy. "I was true at least—oh, true

enough!" he declares, but "Far better commit a fault, and have done— /
As you Dear!—for ever" (79, 91–92). His concluding bitter promise
that "in Paradise / If we meet, I will pass nor turn my face" (113–114)
again invokes the eternal, ironically so in a poem given over to a declara-
tion of transience. "Dis Aliter Visum; Or, le Byron de nos Jours" also
anatomizes a broken relationship, in this case one doomed from the
beginning. An elderly man and a youthful woman love each other, but
the man conceives that any marriage between them would be beset with
insuperable difficulties because of the disparity of age. Ten years later, he
and she are both married to other people, and both their marriages are
failures. The woman, who is the narrator here, accuses the man of cowardice. The moral seems to be that we should not shy away from imperfection because imperfection in this life is our lot and because "a man's
reach should exceed his grasp." Perfection is a sort of death: "what's
whole can increase no more, / Is dwarfed and dies" (141–142). But, as
with any dramatic monologue, we only have the speaker's words to go
by, and the narrator is hardly a disinterested party. Who is to say that
the marriage would have been a success had the man possessed the
courage to embark on it? The context in which this poem appears
implies that any marriage that aims for perfection is doomed before it
even starts. "Too Late," the next poem in the collection, is a similarly
anguished love lyric; the narrator has seen his loved one marry another
man, yet has lived for years in the hope that one day they will be united.
On discovering the woman to be now dead, he rips his jacket to pieces
in his anger ("wreak, like a bull, on the empty coat, / Rage" [44–45]),
but he is equally aware that this mortality marks "courtship made perfect" (140).

The first five poems of *Dramatis Personae*, then, explore questions of
permanence and transience, particularly with respect to love. The connection with Elizabeth Barrett is less that she represented a transient
being and more that Browning himself is uncertain whether his love, a
love he declared as undying, is in fact permanent—whether anything in
the world can be permanent. This in turn opens up a gap between the
mutable present and the afterlife promise of eternal perfection in God.
The eponymous narrator of "Abt Vogler" is meditating on the music he
is himself playing. The music may be transient ("would it might tarry
. . . the beautiful building of mine" [9]), but it puts mankind in touch
with the eternal, the unchanging, "the finger of God . . . existent behind
all laws" (49–50).

> Therefore to whom turn I but to thee, the ineffable Name?
>> Builder and maker, thou, of houses not made with hands!
> What, have fear of change from thee who ever the same?
> . . .
>> The evil is null, is nought, is silence implying sound;
> What was good shall be good, with, for evil, so much good more;
> On the earth the broken arcs; in the heaven, a perfect round.
>> (65–72)

For Vogler music is a metaphor; he himself optimistically asserts that he has found "the C Major of this life," that he is in "harmony" with God.

The apparent spiritual optimism continues in "Rabbi Ben Ezra," with its famous opening:

> Grow old along with me!
>> The best is yet to be,
> The last of life, for which the first was made:
>> Our times are in His hand
>> Who saith "A whole I planned,
> Youth shows but half; trust God: see all nor be afraid!" (1–6)

We seem to be back in the world of Browning the Optimist, "God's in his Heaven— / All's right with the world!" For a collection that starts with such desolate, bleak disillusionment—poems of such power about the transience of love, the breakdown of relationships—this sudden shift in mood may seem startling. And yet there is something curious about this first, much-anthologized stanza. It suggests that "Rabbi Ben Ezra" is going to be a love poem, and it appears to be addressed to a loved one—to a wife, perhaps. Yet the remaining stanzas make no reference at all to a loved one, or even to a secular addressee. Indeed, the end of the poem addresses "God": "Thee, God, who mouldest men; / . . . My times be in Thy hand!" (182–190). And yet, to turn from the end of the poem back to the beginning, it surely cannot be God who is addressed, who is urged, "Grow old along with me!"? What begins as a love lyric transmutes into a hymn, and a philosophical hymn at that, a meditation upon earthly imperfection and the promised perfection of heaven, a consideration of the need to look forward rather than back. If there is something rather chilly about this development, perhaps we ought not to be surprised. For Browning to write, "Grow old along with me! / The best is yet to be," in the aftermath of the premature death of his wife smacks of bitter irony.

Coming as they do after so many poems directly engaged with the evil and miseries of this life, both "Abt Vogler" and "Rabbi Ben Ezra" strike rather hollow notes. To put it baldly, describing evil as "silence implying sound" as Vogler does, or the Rabbi's assertion of "leave the fire ashes, what survives is gold" simply does not give an adequate account of the realities of human suffering. "Rabbi Ben Ezra" is sometimes cited as Browning speaking in his own voice, but it seems to me that few characters in Browning's corpus are less like their creator than the blandly optimistic Ezra—Ezra who has a loving wife to accompany him to old age, who feels general contempt for the common people (the "low kinds" who lack his refined sense of God's plan [17]), who in describing humanity uses a succession of images that increasingly dehumanizes them. He first considers humanity as a "soul" in a "rose-mesh" (62), a description that allows for dignity and a certain self-determination; but he then speaks of "the bird [who] wings and sings" (70), the passive clay on the potter's wheel (151), and a "cup" that exists solely to be "used" (176). Above all, the unwavering certainties of Ezra's position (his belief in "knowledge absolute / Subject to no dispute" [118–119]) sounds very unlike the relativist, liberal Browning.

The figure of Rabbi Ben Ezra has appeared before in Browning's work; he delivers a sermon at the end of "Holy Cross Day" from *Men and Women*. Indeed, several of the poems in *Dramatis Personae* seem to allude directly to earlier Browning. I have already noted that "James Lee's Wife" quotes Browning's 1836 lyric "Still ailing, wind?" by way of commenting on the naïveté of the author. Similarly, various intertextual references in *Dramatis Personae* seem to take earlier positions and modify them with respect to a harder sense of experience and life. It is difficult to recognise Ben Ezra in *Dramatis Personae* as the same figure who appears in *Men and Women*. In "Holy Cross Day," the Rabbi delivers a deathbed speech in which he characterizes the world as "harsh and strange" (69), urging his people to meet with dignity and restraint the barbarities of anti-Semitism: "the torture, prolonged from age to age . . . the branding-tool, the bloody whip, / And the summons to Christian fellowship" (109–114). The almost facile jollity of the Rabbi manifested in "Rabbi Ben Ezra" strikes the reader as simply shallow by comparison. It is presumably no accident that the *Men and Women* poem bespeaks the Rabbi's gloom at the end of his life whereas the *Dramatis Personae* poem has optimistic words coming from the mouth of a young Ben Ezra. The implication must be that experience modifies Ezra's philosophy.

Similarly, the lyric in "James Lee's Wife" called "By the Fireside" seems deliberately to invoke a poem from *Men and Women* that has the same title; but the relationship between the two is one of bitter irony. The narrator of the earlier poem is a man looking back in his old age on a fruitful and blissfully happy marriage to a "perfect wife" (101); the later narrator is sadly recognizing that her marriage is breaking down, her "love's voyage" is sinking, "open hell beneath" (52). It is as if Browning is taking the opportunity to deliberately gloss his earlier collection. When he described the volume to a friend as "a new book of 'Men and Women'" (qtd. in McAleer, 128), he may have meant that *Dramatis Personae* to a certain extent revised or made new the project of the earlier volume.

III. Religious Questions

The question of "certainties," so important a theme in *Dramatis Personae*, has particular resonance for issues of religious faith and doubt. Some of the collection's most enduring poems directly address these issues—"A Death in the Desert" and "Caliban upon Setebos" in particular. The cultural context of these poems was the new intellectual climate of doubt, of scientific skepticism concerning long-held religious and Biblical truths, most famously embodied in Darwin's *Origin of Species* (1859). Whereas Darwin challenged the book of Genesis, two European scholars turned their sights on the life of Christ. David Strauss's *Das Leben Jesu* (1848) and Ernest Renan's *La Vie de Jesus* (1863) both subjected the Gospels to close reading and pointed out a variety of inconsistencies and problems. Neither author was an atheist, and their argument that we should read the Bible as sacred myth rather than as literal truth perhaps does not seem revolutionary today; but at the time, and particularly in the 1860s, their work had a devastating impact. Renan in particular undermined trust in the New Testament by questioning the authenticity of St. John's Gospel and accusing its author of falsifying certain central events relating to the Crucifixion.

In "A Death in the Desert," Browning dramatizes the last days of St. John, picturing him an old man living in a cave in the desert to escape Roman persecution. As if in specific dialogue with skeptics such as

Renan, John talks precisely about the authenticity of his gospel. He agrees that he was not present at the crucifixion, that in effect he cannot vouch for the truth of everything he related. John justifies his position by arguing the difference between faith and proof, and stressing the importance of a strong story to carry the divine revelation from his generation, which actually saw it, to future generations, which will have to rely on testimony:

> No one alive who knew (consider this!)
> —Saw with his eyes and handled with his hands
> That which was from the first, the Word of Life.
> How will it be when none more saith "I saw"? (130–133)

John, *contra* Renan, presents himself as an authentic witness because he "[s]aw with his eyes and handled with his hands" the source of Christianity, Christ himself. But what he was able to know firsthand subsequent generations will have to take at secondhand; they (and we) are removed from the central, divine event.

In fact, as the form of "A Death in the Desert" makes plain, our position is further removed than even secondhand. The poem, which purports to be the text of John's last speech before his death, is framed with a series of other narrators and bibliographic annotations, and these frames enact the problems of textual transmission that are at the heart of the work. Browning might easily have printed John's last speech as a separate monologue, a poem in which the narrator would be John himself. But he chose not to. If we ask who the narrator actually is, we run into difficulties: he introduces himself in the opening lines of the poem with circumspection, saying, "I may not write [my name]" for fear of persecution, giving us only his initials ("M.E."). Moreover, this unnamed narrator was not actually present when John made his final speech; he inherited the manuscript of the speech from his wife's uncle Xanthus. But Xanthus wasn't the one who recorded the speech; that was done by "Pamphylax the Antiochene." In other words, this text is profoundly contingent—each narrator depends upon another—and there is a powerful sense of belatedness, of missing the main event, which is actually the chief theme of the work. If we want to assure ourselves of the truth of Christianity via this manuscript, we need to be sure of the reliability of the narrator, M.E. But M.E. is contingent upon Xanthus, and Xanthus upon Pamphylax, and Pamphylax upon St. John, and St. John upon Christ. Even Christ is not the central truth, but rather an adjunct, a figure contingent upon God the Father. Religious truth comes to us not just secondhand, but from many hands, at the end of a long chain of transmission. This process makes any notion of absolute certainty extremely problematic.

That "Caliban upon Setebos" is also a religious poem written in dialogue with contemporary theological debates is signaled by its subtitle, "Natural Theology in the Island." The reference is to the work of theologian William Paley's *Natural Theology, or, Evidences of the Existence and Attributes of the Deity, Collected from the Appearances of Nature* (1802), the work that gave the world the famous "God-as-watchmaker" argument. The argument goes something like this: when we look into the complex innards of a watch, we know that there must have been a watchmaker who made the device; similarly, the world is too complex and beautiful to have arisen by chance and must therefore have been created. However limited Paley's arguments may seem today, they carried a great deal of weight with many of Browning's contemporaries. In this monologue, Caliban, the bestial character from Shakespeare's *Tempest*, acts as a sort of primitive Paley, which is to say he looks at the natural world of his island and intuits the existence of a god (called "Setebos") from its attributes. What is not clear, however, is whether the thrust of this monologue is a celebration of the necessity of the deity (since even so brutal a creature as Caliban recognizes that God exists) or an attack upon Paleyesque or (as many argue) Calvinist theology. For Caliban the world is a frightening, miserable, and painful place; he consequently imagines that God must be a frightening being, delighting in inflicting misery and pain. The gap between this conception of the deity and Browning's own liberal-humanist Christian god of infinite love and forgiveness is too large to be crossed. Caliban makes God in his own image, transfers his own imperfections, suitably enlarged, onto his godhead; Browning, on the other hand, consistently stressed that precisely because humanity is imperfect God must be the only perfect being. Browning's God is a very different entity from Setebos.

Actually, Browning seems to be both criticizing the limited theology that insists upon a god of jealousy and pain, and celebrating his own more abstract notions of God's perfection. Caliban imagines Setebos as an unhappy god, "ill at ease" because "He cannot change His cold, / Nor cure its ache" (31–33). But at the same time Caliban imagines another, higher entity, "something over Setebos /That made Him" (129–130). While Setebos rages at his own relative impotence, this upper god, whom Caliban calls "the Quiet," is omnipotent: "This Quiet, all it hath a mind to, doth" (137). The pantheon of "Caliban upon Setebos" imagines two gods, one made in the image of Caliban, the other made in the image of Browning, or at least Browning's ability to conceive abstract and ultimate perfection.

Still, it is difficult to avoid the feeling that "Caliban upon Setebos" is designed as a critique of the position of Paley and those theologians who advance the "argument from design." If the logic of Paley is followed, Browning seems to be suggesting, it leads not to Calvinism (as several critics have asserted) but to another of Browning's favorite religious targets, the excesses of medieval Roman Catholicism.

Caliban is not a rational or thinking being in any profound capacity; his reasoning is based on his senses. The poem opens with him wallowing in the mud in the heat of midday, soaking up his sensual pleasure (and talking about himself in the third person):

> Will sprawl, now that the heat of day is best,
> Flat on his belly in the pit's much mire,
> With elbows wide, fists clenched to prop his chin.
> And while he kicks both feet in the cool slush,
> And feels about his spine small eft-things course,
> Run in and out each arm, and make him laugh. (1–6)

Caliban lives for his senses, and as his sensual pleasure is fleeting and sensual deprivation and suffering are frequent, he fashions his god in this manner. His religion is sensual, rather than abstract or intellectual.

When he senses his god is displeased (when the weather at the end of the poem changes for the worse), his immediate instinct is to mortify his flesh—to bite his lip and promise to starve himself:

> Fool to gibe at Him!
> Lo! 'Lieth flat and loveth Setebos
> 'Maketh his teeth meet through his upper lip,
> Will let those quails fly, will not eat this month. (291–294)

This urge to punish the flesh in order to appease a wrathful god was, Browning thought, a function of a sensual age, such as medieval Catholicism. When times were good, medieval people lived for pleasure;

when times were bad, they attempted to mollify God by abstaining from pleasure or by mortifying the flesh. The point, according to Browning, is that the argument from design is based upon the corporeal world, the world of the senses; any god intuited from such an argument will be a corporeal, sensual god. For Browning, such a god was a symptom of a more primitive age of humanity (Caliban is a representative of this less advanced state of society, and possibly, in the wake of the debate over evolution that followed the publication of Darwin's *Origin of Species*, an earlier version of man, a "missing link").

As the "Epilogue" to *Dramatis Personae* makes plain, religion for Browning is something that evolves and improves as mankind evolves and improves. In the "Epilogue" we have three speakers; the first is from the time of King David, for whom religion literally depends upon miracles (God appearing as a pillar of cloud). The second is a contemporary of Browning's, one who judges religion by rational, scientific criteria. But the third speaker is able to grasp the true state of affairs, that God depends neither upon supernatural displays nor scientific reasoning; in fact, God does not depend upon nature at all—though the play of nature "dance / About each man of us, retire, advance" like a "pageant," belief nonetheless depends upon the "heart" (not the head) of the individual.

> That one Face, far from vanish, rather grows
> Or decomposes but to recompose,
> Become my universe that feels and knows! (99–101)

The lyric "Confessions," in which a dying man prompted by a priest recalls but cannot regret a youthful love affair, is chiefly remembered for its final stanza:

> [We] stood by the rose-wreathed gate. Alas,
>   We loved, sir—used to meet:
> How sad and bad and mad it was—
>   But then, how it was sweet! (33–36)

But in a sense a more interesting aspect of the poem is the way the narrator latches onto the objects ranged on his bedside table to represent his past. He sees "where the physic bottles stand / On the table's edge" as a "suburb lane" on the grounds that "the lane sloped much as the bottles do"; the blue curtain he can see becomes "the old June weather / Blue above lane and wall," and "that farthest bottle labelled 'Ether'" is his lover's house "o'ertopping all" (6–16). The narrator seems to be participating in the sort of language game that the later Wittgenstein would have recognized. The premise is one of the arbitrariness of signifiers in the world of the imagination. Browning is exploring the way meaning (not the meaning of individual words any more than the "meaning" of religion) is not somehow magically inscribed, not transcendentally "fixed." For Browning, meaning is derived by the heart, in an emotionally faithful extrapolation, and not by the head.

"Mr Sludge 'the Medium'" is the longest poem in *Dramatis Personae* by a long stretch. Indeed, at 1,525 lines it is longer than some poems Browning published in volumes by themselves (for instance, *La Saisiaz*, *Agamemnon*). The sheer length of the piece is at first sight rather puzzling in that it purports to be a satirical attack on a self-professed spiritualist and medium, a fake who bamboozles people with table-rapping and other "communications" with the afterlife. Surely such a target could be disposed of more swiftly? One-and-a-half thousand lines of dense, difficult verse aimed at such a pettifogging figure is taking a poetic sledgehammer to crack a particularly tiny nut. More puzzling still is the fact that Mr. Sludge himself is based upon a real man, Daniel Dunglas Home, a medium that both Robert and Elizabeth had met in 1855 (the name "Sludge" recalls the chief element in this figure's middle name—"Dung"). Robert had despised Home from the first, but Elizabeth had been wholly taken in by his charade; she was captivated by all such supernatural claptrap. Surely the expenditure of this amount of poetic energy attacking Home meant that Browning was, unavoidably, attacking his late wife's interests and therefore Elizabeth herself?

The answer, of course, is that a superbly vigorous and vitriolic attack on mediums, spiritualism, and the whole bag-and-baggage of the trade is only part of Browning's purpose. Although "Mr Sludge" begins as a straightforward explanation of how a medium begins his cheating career, how people collude in their own deception and so on—it eventually develops into a much more complex exploration of the relationship between life and death. Sludge addresses the relationship between youth and age (using, significantly, many of the same images and much of the vocabulary of "Rabbi Ben Ezra," although to very different ends) and sees age as nothing but a diminution, a fading away. We are planted like seedlings, but "you shot up and frost nipped you off" (1362); the most you can boast is that you might have grown to be a magnificent tree in "in other climes":

> Young, you've force
> Wasted like well-streams: old,—oh, then indeed,
> Behold a labyrinth of hydraulic pipes
> Through which you'd play off wondrous waterwork;
> Only no water's left to feed their play. (1367–1371)

When young you have a "spark"; but when you grow old and attempt to light a fire with it, you discover that "it's extinct" (1378). The contrast with the other speakers of *Dramatis Personae*—who all agree that the spark comes into its own in old age or, as St. John believes, at death—is marked and deliberate. Sludge constructs a "pasteboard" afterlife (1392), his imagination too impoverished to conceive of a real one. Because he possesses all the skills of the talented storyteller he leads people away from the truth: "you find you're in a flock," he promises, "Of the youthful, earnest, passionate. . . . Participate in Sludgehood . . . banish doubt, / And modesty and reticence and modesty alike!" (1423–1430).

Browning's anger is not so much directed at Elizabeth's old passion for occult beliefs (as Daniel Karlin points out, Browning had plenty of interests in supernatural and arcane areas of knowledge)[2] as at the pretence that a person can communicate with a dead loved one—that he, say, could communicate with Elizabeth—as if that person were still living. Browning was convinced that the soul survived death, but he was also convinced that death involved passing into a realm of existence so much more perfect and complete than this one that it is not possible for us access it without dying first. When Elizabeth next appears in Browning's verse, for instance, it is as a superhuman "lyric Love, half-angel and half-bird," the dedicatee and muse of Browning's mightiest poetic undertaking, *The Ring and the Book*.

Chapter Seven
The Ring and the Book
1868–1869

One day in June 1860, the Piazza San Lorenzo, in Florence, having been converted for the day into a giant market, was crowded with dozens of rickety wooden tables selling all manner of "odds and ends": "bronze angel-heads once knobs attached to chests," "tribes of tongs, shovels in sheaves," "cast clothes a-sweetening in the sun" (*Ring and the Book*, 1.55–108). Rummaging among the junk, Browning came across a vellum-covered book made up of a variety of printed and manuscript materials. These were legal documents relating to a trial that had taken place in Rome in 1698 in which it was charged that an Italian nobleman, crazed with sexual jealousy (shades of "My Last Duchess") and convinced that his teenage wife had been having an affair with the local priest, had hired a band of cutthroats and killed the girl along with her mother and father. It was bloody, grisly material, precisely the sort of subject matter that critics had tut-tutted at in Browning's earlier work. He bought the volume ("The Old Yellow Book," as it is now known) for one lire: eight pence in old English money, 3p in modern British tender. Rarely can a book lover have made a better bargain.

Elizabeth, growing more and more ill, was rather disgusted with the sordidness of the story; she could in no way share Browning's enthusiasm for it. Convinced that the material in the Old Yellow Book would make excellent literature, Browning was perhaps unwilling to write it up himself in the face of his wife's hostility; it seems that during 1860 and 1861 he sent the story to a variety of contemporary writers. He offered it to the historian W. C. Cartwright, then to the romantic novelist Miss Ogle, then Tennyson, and finally the novelist Anthony Trollope. They all turned the offer down. Browning's initial resistance to utilizing this source material himself rather suggests he was influenced by Elizabeth's hostility to so sordid a subject matter; but if this was indeed the case, then his eventual decision to write *The Ring and the Book* cannot but be seen as an example, like "Mr Sludge" or the later "Prince Hohenstiel-Schwangau," of Browning turning against his wife's influence.

The question of provenance is very much to the point, given the prominence of the whole adventure of discovery in the first book of the epic. Browning flaunts the personal relevance of the story by flourishing first the ring (it was a real ring, worn by Browning and engraved with the Italian *Vis Mea*, "My Strength") and then the Old Yellow Book, which Browning twirls before our eyes with a certain insouciance:

> Do you see this square old yellow Book, I toss
> I' the air and catch again, and twirl about
> By the crumpled vellum covers,—pure crude fact
> Secreted from man's life when hearts beat hard,
> And brains, high-blooded, ticked two centuries since?
> Examine it yourselves! (1.33–38)

The dichotomy between beating hearts and ticking brains, between spirit and law, faith and proof, is one of the key thematic relations of the poem as a whole. More immediately, Browning goes on to relate precisely where and how he found his source material, and he ends the first book with a wry address to the "British Public, ye who like me not, / (God love you!)" and an invocation to the presiding spirit of his dead wife, "O lyric Love, half-angel and half-bird" (1.1391). The effect is to root the whole epic firmly in an elaborately personal myth of poetic origin.

There is nothing unusual, of course, about a poet beginning his or her work with an invocation to the Muse (in this case, Elizabeth Barrett); but for so private a poet as Browning to be so open about the personal provenance and (inescapably) the personal relevance of the matter of his epic is strange. It is difficult to avoid the parallels between the events of the poem (spiritual young woman trapped in a house with an oppressive man, rescued by a spiritual young man, and carried off to Rome to bear her child) and the events of Browning's own recent life (poetic middle-aged woman trapped in house with an oppressive man, rescued by a poetic young man, and carried off to Florence to bear her child). By in effect foregrounding the personal, Browning makes an identification almost inevitable; even the title he chose, *The Ring and the Book*, reflects his own initials and recalls his earlier admission to Elizabeth Barrett that his ambition had been to write "R.B. A Poem."

I. R.B. a Poem

The Ring and the Book was published in four monthly parts from November 1868 to February 1869, with three complete monologues (or books) in each installment. Written in blank verse, its 12 books and 21,116 lines make it a massive work by any standard, although (as Carlyle pointed out) it was "all spun out of a story but a few lines long" that "only wanted forgetting." Each of the poem's books is a lengthy dramatic monologue, and in the course of the work ten speakers give their various and partial perspectives. In other words, the structure of the work involves telling the same story over and over again; it is a testament to Brownings massive inventiveness that our interest never flags.

In Book 1, "The Ring and the Book," the narrator (identified with but presumably not identical to Browning himself) describes in turn the ring and the book of his title. The ring is introduced as a metaphor for the process of literary creation—in particular the forging of a literary artifact out of an alloy composed of the artist's imagination and "pure crude fact." The book signifies both the Old Yellow Book and the book we are reading, as well as an emblem of textuality: "small-quarto size, part print part manuscript: / A book in shape but, really, pure crude fact." There is little attempt to preserve narrative mystery; in translating the Latin title of the Old Yellow Book, Browning effectively maps out the whole story:

> A Roman murder-case:
> Position of the entire criminal cause
> Of Guido Franceschini, nobleman,
> With certain Four the cutthroats in his pay,
> Tried, all five, and found guilty and put to death
> By heading or by hanging as befitted ranks,
> At Rome on February Twenty Two,
> Since our salvation Sixteen Ninety Eight:
> Wherein it is disputed if, and when,
> Husbands may kill adulterous wives, yet 'scape
> The customary forfeit. (1.121–131)

Much of the remainder of Book 1 is concerned with outlining the (factual) details of the murder and anticipating the various speakers who will come forward. The circumstances are as follows: Count Guido, an impoverished Arezzo nobleman and minor churchman, married Pompilia, the young daughter of an elderly Roman couple, in the mistaken belief that she was wealthy. At the beginning of the marriage, the parents lived with Guido and Pompilia in Arezzo, but the marriage was unhappy, and the parents (Pietro and Violante) soon returned to Rome. Once there they sued Guido for the return of Pompilia's dowry, revealing that she was an illegitimate child (Violante having bought her from a prostitute and passed her off as her own). Eventually, an utterly miserable Pompilia fled her husband's house in the company of a young priest, Caponsacchi, and was pursued by Guido. Arrested on the outskirts of Rome, the priest was sent into internal exile for three years and the (pregnant) Pompilia taken to a nunnery while the lawsuits were decided. At the time of her confinement, however, Pompilia was released into the care of her putative parents. Two weeks after the birth of her son, Guido and his accomplices burst into their house, murdered the old couple, and stabbed Pompilia repeatedly, wounding her fatally. Arrested for this crime, Guido claimed justifiable homicide on the grounds of what he insisted was his wife's adultery with the priest, Caponsacchi. Despite his plea, conviction followed, and Guido then pleaded exemption on behalf of his (lowly) status in the Church. The Pope eventually ruled, however, that Guido was guilty, and he was executed.

The speaker of Book 2, "Half-Rome," is an ordinary Roman man. He expresses his sympathy for the husband, arguing that Guido was an honest man who had grown old waiting for a promised preferment in the Church: he had been easy prey for the wicked old couple. The result of Violante's scheming was that "Guido's broad back was saddled to bear all— / Pietro, Violante, and Pompilia too." (ii.391–392) His wicked parents-in-law had no sooner rid themselves of their daughter than they tried to snatch back the dowry, and Pompilia began an affair with the local priest. When Guido tried to obtain justice he was rebuffed in the courts, and when he heard of the birth of a boy—a boy who would be falsely presented as an heir—his patience gave way to rage. It becomes apparent during the course of the monologue that "Half-Rome" is hardly a representative figure. We realize that the narrator is himself a husband and that he considers his own wife to be wayward, even adulterous. If he argues that Guido's actions were "the better for you and me and all the world, / Husbands of wives, especially in Rome" (ii.1538–1539), it is because he has half a mind to use the knife he flourishes during the monologue (ii.67) to similarly punish "a certain what's-his-name and jackanapes / Somewhat too civil" about the house "where I keep a wife" (ii.1544–1546). In other words, the view "Half-Rome" has of the situation is hardly unprejudiced.

Book 3, "The Other Half-Rome" exhibits similar partiality in judgment. This speaker is a bachelor who is chiefly moved by pity for the stabbed Pompilia ("A flower-like body, to frighten at a bruise / You'd think, yet now, stabbed through and through again") (iii.5–6) and her dead parents. He argues that Guido was a brute of a husband and Pompilia quite right to try and escape. Guido had no business appealing to the law in the first place; he had no right "flying out of court" crying "'Honour's hurt the sword must cure!'" when the process did not go his way. "The Other Half-Rome" seems to have no particular axe to grind, but by the end of the monologue we realize that he is actually personally involved. He mentions the "lie that was . . . imputed me" by Guido during some law case or other ("When [Guido] objected to my contract's clause" [iii.1685]). Just as "Half-Rome"'s sympathy for Guido seemed predicated upon his own experience with a flighty wife, so "The Other Half-Rome" seems to oppose Guido for personal reasons rather than because of any disinterested sense of justice.

Book 4's "Tertium Quid" ("third quantity") provides a more balanced because less personally involved perspective. This speaker is attending a high-class soiree and promises the assembled notaries and ecclesiastics "a reasoned statement of the case" rather than the coarse "gossip-guess" of the mob (4.920–926). Specifically addressing a "Highness" and an "Excellency," he is careful not to offend the prejudices of either; consequently he sees no reason to assume that wrong is entirely on either side, and his summing up is indeed fairly balanced, although there is an undoubted class prejudice in favor of the noble-born Guido over the commoner Pompilia.

In Book 5, "Count Guido Franceschini," Guido addresses the Court, having confessed under torture to his crime. He tries to elicit sympathy for his injuries (his shoulder has been pulled out of its socket on the rack: "aie, aie, aie, / Not your fault, sweet Sir! . . . the shoulder blade, / The left one, that seems wrong i' the socket," [5.9–17]), and his speech is characterized by a mixture of sycophancy and self-pity. He makes great play with certain alleged love letters between Pompilia and Caponsacchi, and with the fact that he whispered the name "Caponsacchi" at the door on the night of the murder. If his wife had not been the priest's lover, he insists, she would not have opened the door at the sound of his name.

Book 6, "Giuseppe Caponsacchi," has the priest telling his side of the story. He confesses his love for Pompilia but insists that it was pure and chaste. He helped her escape her monstrous husband out of compassion and for no carnal reason. One of the most striking aspects of Caponsacchi's monologue, in contrast to the oily sycophancy of Guido's, is the priest's barely- (and sometimes un-) suppressed anger. He is furious at Guido's brutality toward the child-wife "young, tall, beautiful, strange, and sad" (6.399), particularly as he considers Pompilia to have been an embodiment of his own spiritual salvation. He claims that Pompilia had taught him "to live . . . and learn by her . . . to do with nothing but the true, / The good, the eternal" (6.2085–2089). In regard to Guido, Caponsacchi's anger splutters and boils over in muscular, writhing verse, often characterized with slithering sibilants and clogging consonants, as when he imagines Guido finally in Hell and meeting that arch-traitor, Judas Iscariot:

> Kiss him the kiss, Iscariot! Pay that back,
> That smatch o' the slaver blistering on your lip—
> By the better trick, the insult he spared Christ—
> Lure him the lure o' the letters, Arentine [i.e., Guido]!
> Lick him o'er slimy-smooth with jelly-filth
> O' the verse-and-prose pollution in love's guise!
> The cockatrice is with the basilisk!
> There let them grapple, denizens of the dark,
> Foes or friends, but indissolubly bound,
> In their one spot out of the ken of God
> Or care of man, for ever and ever more! (6.1944–1954)

Wonderful stuff. The religious iconography is relevant not only because Guido had earlier tried comparing himself to the martyr of martyrs, Christ, but also because the overarching conviction of *The Ring and the Book* is that ultimate truth is found only with God. It also foreshadows the representation in the next Book of the dying Pompilia as an earthly type of the Virgin Mary.

In Book 7, speaking from her deathbed, Pompilia asserts her innocence. She was never Caponsacchi's lover except in a spiritual and pure
sense; the love letters supposedly from her to the priest are forgeries, for
she cannot even read and write. Indeed, considering that she is lying on
a bed perishing of multiple stab wounds, her equanimity and ability to
forgive (she happily forgives Guido his crime, for instance) are remarkable to the point of disbelief. She dies declaring that God shows "His
light / For us i' the dark to rise by. And I rise" (7.1845). In a sense, the
problem in her characterization is the same one that affects Milton's *Paradise Lost*: traits of purity and distance do not make for engaging literary
creations. Just as Milton's evil and scheming figure of Satan is much
more interesting than his figure of God, Guido's grotesque but vivid
and energetic self-presentation is much more powerful than the rather
weak reiteration of forgiveness and goodness that constitute "Pompilia."

Book 8 ("Dominus Hyacinthus de Archangelis") and Book 9 ("Juris
Doctor Johannes-Baptista Bottinius") portray the speeches of the
Court's legal advocates, the former speaking on Guido's behalf, the latter on Pompilia's. Each an example of colossal legal quibbling and
pedantry, both are represented as being equally beside the point. A
rather different sort of "lawyer," or legal judge, emerges in Book 10,
"The Pope." The trial has condemned Guido, and he has appealed to the
Pope. From dawn until dark, the Pope has been studying the facts of the
case, and his attempt to reach an authoritative judgment causes him to
interrogate his deepest assumptions about God, humanity, and religion.
But, ultimately, Gudio's action cannot be defended, and the Pope
refuses to intercede.

Book 11, "Guido," effectively puts paid to any sense of "relativism"
in the poem's overall moral scheme. Guido's second monologue sees him
in his prison cell, and in the course of it his conciliatory mask slips to
reveal a ferocious, unrepentant figure. There can no longer be any doubt
of his guilt in legal or moral terms. He announces that he has always
hated the "timid chalky ghost" who was his wife. He may have thought
he loved her once, but now his distaste is violent: "I grow one gorge / To
loathingly reject Pompilia's pale / Poison my hasty hunger took for
food" (12.2402–2404). The image of him vomiting up Pompilia cuts
both ways, of course: it suggests that Pompilia has ruined Guido, but it
also reinforces the negative picture of Guido that emerges from the
images of predation occurring throughout the work, in particular the
repeated characterizations of Guido as wolf and Pompilia as lamb (*wolf*
and *lamb* also have religious resonance, of course). Finally, the cowardice

underlying Guido's brutality becomes apparent when, hearing the steps of the executioners on the stairs outside his cell, he breaks down and begs for his life:

> Life is all!
>
> I was just stark mad,—let the madman live
> Pressed by as many chains as you please pile!
> Don't open! Hold me from them! I am yours,
> I am the Granduke's—no, I am the Pope's!
> Abate,—Cardinal,—Christ,—Maria,—God, . . .
> Pompilia, will you let them murder me? (11.2419–2425)

As its title suggests, Book 12 ("The Book and the Ring") closes the hermeneutic circle opened up at the poem's beginning. The narrator concludes with several letters from contemporaries describing subsequent events—Guido's execution, the Pope's restoration of Pompilia's "perfect fame"—and various details of the political situation in the Rome of 1692. The book ends with another dedication to the "Lyric Love."

Browning interrogates issues of truth, love, law, and language. "Truth" is perhaps the central issue, and since truth is something that needs to be determined, or interpreted, *The Ring and the Book* becomes in effect a gigantic hermeneutic epic, arguably the first great epistemological poem. But seeing the poem in these terms, however valid such a critical perspective is (and however often critics have brought this sort of analysis to it) runs the risk of overlooking the supreme humanity of Browning's achievement. As portraits of character and as recreations of a historical period, these monologues have few equals, in the nineteenth century or elsewhere. Certainly it was on these grounds that contemporaries praised the work and praised it highly. The *Athenaeum* for instance declared that *The Ring and the Book* was "beyond all parallel the supremest poetical achievement of our time . . . the most precious and profound spiritual treasure that England has produced since the days of Shakespeare."[1] Viewing literature as "spiritual treasure" may strike an odd note today, but it was the keystone of Victorian admiration for the undertaking.

It is remarkable that the Victorian and the postmodern age, with two very different notions as to what constitutes good art, can both agree on the greatness of *The Ring and the Book*. But, then again, the balance between opposites is, in a sense, the great strength of this work. It does not go too far to suggest that the key mode of this epic is "half-and-half." Just as Elizabeth Barrett is wife and Muse, "half-angel and half-bird" (1.1391), so the poem as a whole is half true and half fiction; like the gold alloy that makes up Elizabeth's ring, it is a blend of "pure crude fact" and the poet's strengthening imagination. This half-and-half framework highlights a variety of carefully mediated oppositions. Priesthood and sexuality, for instance, are of central concern in the book. Guido is kind of a priest (half-priest, we might say), although clearly incapable of the priestly vow of celibacy. (Catholic priests do not normally marry, as Guido does; he is able to do so because he is the lowest rank of churchman.) Caponsacchi, on the other hand, is a priest proper, and for him the question of sexuality is more complicated. Although both Pompilia and Caponsacchi deny that there was any sex between them, there is an undeniably strong erotic undercurrent to their escape together. Pompilia, describing Caponsacchi as "more a woman than a man" (7.549), may intend to absolve him of lust toward her, but in fact this blurring of the boundaries between genders actually focuses our attention more directly on his sexual status; it is even unsettling in a hermaphrodite sense. Moreover, if Caponsacchi is half man and half woman, he is also by virtue of his religious position as an intercessor half man and half God. The gap between God and the world is too great (here as elsewhere in Browning), and the need for a bridge very great: "We want such intermediary race / To make communication possible; / The real thing were too lofty, we too low" (11.1937–1939). In other words, Caponsacchi embodies the mediating thrust of Browning's poetic project, the balancing of opposites, the synthesis of contraries. And behind these more literal half-and-halves lie the various thematic binary oppositions that structure the poem: male/female, good/evil, false/true, inside/outside. Browning's masterwork mediates these sorts of polarities and uses them to create its subtle, allusive, and shifting textual fabric.

II. *The Ring and the Book* and Modern Theory

As the greatest nineteenth-century textual exploration of, and indeed embodiment of, relativism, *The Ring and the Book* has been eagerly taken up by relativist and deconstructionist literary scholars. W. David Shaw goes so far as to declare that "problems associated with contemporary deconstruction and hermeneutics were familiar to Browning and already understood by him" in *The Ring and the Book*; and E. Warwick Slinn argues that the poem marks "the triumph of dialectical thinking" and the moment when the unified Romantic sense of "self" can be seen "giving way to Derridean *différance*, to a weaving without totality."[2] The case for a deconstructionist Browning is certainly an appealing one, and the basic premises of *The Ring and the Book* do seem to support the notion that, however much Browning may have believed in a transcendental and essentialist "truth" in God, he was only too aware that truth in this world is always contingent, always partial, always a product of shifting cultural and textual forces. A passage from Caryle's essay "On History" (1830), which may have directly influenced Browning and certainly sheds light on the construction of *The Ring and the Book*, is relevant here:

> Nay, even with regard to those occurrences which do stand recorded, which, at their origin, have seemed worthy of record, and the summary of which constitutes what we now call History, is not our understanding of them altogether incomplete? The old story of Sir Walter Raleigh's looking from his prison-window, on some street tumult, which afterwards three witnesses reported in three different ways, himself differing from them all, is still a true lesson for us all.[3]

The situation described seems very close to that of *The Ring and the Book* and seems to lead us toward a thoroughly relativistic perspective. But there is an important difference between Carlyle's instance and Browning's masterpiece. In the Sir Walter Raleigh anecdote there is no way of determining which of the four witnesses is closest to the truth, or indeed if any of them are. In fact, "truth" is quite irrecoverable in this case. This is the more Derridean situation. But in *The Ring and the Book* the point is not that ten witnesses will all vary from the "truth" to a lesser or greater extent, but that the person with the overview (in this case, Browning himself) will at least be able to serve as a benchmark. Derrida might argue that there is no recoverable objective truth at all. All ten are equally false, or true; and that the extent to which we are able to assign qualities such as "true" or "false" wholly depends, is wholly relative.

Yet this extreme leveling of value is not what we find in *The Ring and the Book*. At the end of this massive textual undertaking, Book 12 does not suggest, but insists upon our argument:

> —I demand assent
> To the enunciation of my text

> In face of one proof more that "God is true
> And every man a liar"—that who trusts
> To human testimony for a fact
> Gets this sole fact—himself is proved a fool;
> Man's speech is false . . .
> And . . . truth seems reserved for heaven. (12.598–607)

Browning may allow the relativist point that "every man [is] a liar," but he is equally adamant not just that "God is truth" but that it is possible to approach closer to truth in an undeniable, objectively supportable manner. The various witnesses in *The Ring and the Book* disagree on various small points, but there is no doubt of the main facts of the case. Guido is guilty as charged; indeed, he is more than guilty—he is diabolical, a man-beast, the worst of villains. Pompilia is innocent and more—so pure, so spiritual, and so fine a creature that she is almost a saint. By the same token, Caponsacchi is a hotheaded but honorable man; the lawyers are foolish irrelevancies; and the Pope is a wise judge. The law case actually hinges on the question "if, and when, Husbands may kill adulterous wives." Again, and although various speakers have various views on this matter, we, as readers, never doubt that it is wrong to kill your wife, whether she is adulterous or not. The relativism of *The Ring and the Book* is maintained safely within a larger area—a ring, we might say—of absolute certainty. In Browning's conception, God rings the ordinary world like the sky surrounds the earth.

The distinction here is between inside and outside. On the one hand we have the (negatively portrayed) characters who are obsessed with the internal: Archangelis's obsession with food, Guido's repeated references in his first monologue to his physical pains and twinges and in his second to the agonies of his thwarted ego (his "angry heart explodes"; he's "combustion-ripe" [11.466]), his rhetoric of devouring and predation. By contrast, the "good" characters look outward and upward, to others rather than to the self, and ultimately to God. Pompilia talks of herself "rising" through the sky to God; in contrast to the stifling, subterranean, dungeon imagery of Guido, her monologue is characterized by images of the sky and clouds. The Pope is close to death and remarkably unegotistical; he strives to judge according to absolute values rather than political or personal ones. He too looks forward to the afterlife and he uses the sky to furnish him with an image of the truth:

> I stood at Naples once, a night so dark
> I could have scarce conjectured there was earth
> Anywhere, sky or sea or world at all:
> But the night's black was burst through by a blaze—
> . . .
> There lay the city thick and plain with spires,
> And, like a ghost disshrouded, white the sea.
> So may the truth be flashed out by one blow. (10.2118–2127)

The whole of *The Ring and the Book*, in fact, follows this particular trajectory—from the grisly church vault holding the stabbed and mangled corpses of Pietro and Violante at the opening of "Half-Rome"'s monologue, to the soaring peroration at the beginning of the final book, where the course of events is compared to a firework:

> Thus, lit and launched, up and up roared and soared
> A rocket, till the key o' the vault was reached
> And wide heaven held, a breathless minute-space,
> In brilliant usurpature. (12.2–5)

The Pope and the other "good" characters (including the narrator of the first book) all adhere to this hierarchical, absolutist, God-oriented pattern. The real relativists, or deconstructionists, in *The Ring and the Book* are the two lawyers and Guido—the latter in particular, with his acute sense of "artistry's haunting curse, the Incomplete!" (11.1559).

But it is perhaps difficult to see how hermeneutics, the business of interpretation, can ever establish certainty; how can we be sure, for instance, of Guido's guilt or Pompilia's innocence? This kind of question is of primary importance not only for *The Ring and the Book* but for the dramatic monologue as a genre. We are invited to assess, and judge, the speaker of any dramatic monologue; this is doubly true of *The Ring and the Book*, where we follow the progress of a trial, something specifically convened for the purposes of judgment. How can it be that our judgments (Guido's guilt, Pompilia's innocent) are accurate and unbiased?

It is an obvious although rarely noticed point about *The Ring and the Book*—indeed, I assume it has been so rarely noted only because it is so obvious—that this text is constructed around the interplay between two separate models of judgment (or hermeneutics). The distinction is made between legal (or institutional) and personal (or human) interpretation and judgment: which is to say, there is the way the law reads, assesses, and judges situations on the one hand, and there is the way human beings instinctually, empathetically deal with circumstances on the other.

Browning's opinion of lawyers seems not to have been high. Writing to his friend Julia Wedgwood, he describes Archangelis and Bottinus as "buffoons":

> As for the lawyers, why, *Who* is going to find fault with me, in the other world, for writing about what *I*, at least, wish had never been made? But made they are, and just so . . . just so, I have known them . . . I hate the lawyers: and confess to tasting . . . satisfaction, as I emphasise their buffoonery. (quoted in Richard Curle, 177)

Why does he hate lawyers so potently, we might ask ourselves? They are only doing their job. Indeed, *The Ring and the Book* shows the system of law to work, at least insofar as Guido is convicted of his crimes. Moreover, it is Guido who is most virulently opposed to the system of law, since his own attempt to have the courts condemn Pompilia and disinherit her child had come to nothing. In his second monologue he insists that it was the inadequacy of the legal system that led him to take the law into his own hands, to kill of Pompilia:

> [I] plucked at law's robe a-rustle through the courts,
>
> . . .
>
> Procedures to no purpose! Then flashed truth!
> The letter kills, the spirit keeps alive
> In law and gospel: there be nods and winks
> Instruct a wise man to assist himself. (11.1525–1531)

If I am going to argue that, in his own way, Browning advocates that "the letter kills, the spirit keeps alive," then I clearly need to distinguish Browning's position from Guido's. The main distinction is epistemological. Guido's dislike of lawyers has nothing to do with truth, only with expediency and his own dire straits. Browning consistently advocates an epiphanic conception of truth. "Then flashed truth!": the "truth" flashes upon you, suddenly and blindingly. I have already quoted the Pope's closing hope that "the truth be flashed out by one blow" (10.2126);

Pompilia similarly talks about the truth of "God's instant" (7.1841). And Browning himself, describing how he planned the complicated and inwrought structure of *The Ring and the Book*, uses the same rhetoric of spontaneous revelation. "I went this morning to see the mountain pass called 'Le pas de Roland,'" he wrote to Julia Wedgwood in 1864, "—the tradition being that he opened a way through a rock that effectually blocks it up, by one kick of his boot, and so let Charlemagne's army pass." As if inspired by Roland's single breakthough "kick," Browning (so he later claimed) laid out "the full plan of his twelve cantos" then and there, using pebbles to represent the books and arranging them in a circle. (quoted in Curle, 63). Myths of creation, as I have argued, are of particular and personal importance to Browning, so this assertion is particularly interesting.

Spontaneity, then, is valorized. We might think back to so early a work as "My Last Duchess," with its evident parallels to *The Ring and the Book*: it is oriented entirely around the natural spontaneity of the Duchess and the evil desire of the Duke to stifle such immediacy, to banish all possibility of spontaneous action from his wife by replacing her with an artifact. Similarly, in *The Ring and the Book*, spontaneous action is consistently presented in a good light. Caponsacchi, speaking of his rescue of Pompilia, says that he did not give the matter a great deal of thought ("'Thought'? nay, Sirs, what shall follow was not thought" [6.937]), and Pompilia recollects how the priest pledged himself, without preliminaries, to her with all his heart:

> He replied—
> The first word I heard ever from his lips,
> All himself in it,—an eternity
> Of speech to match the immeasurable depths
> O' the soul that then broke silence—"I am yours."
> (7.1442–1447)

Lawyers like Archangelis, however, laboriously plod through lengthy quotations from Latin, translating each phrase as it comes out. Bottinius works hard on his speech, even practicing it in the solitude of his rooms (1.1202); but he in particular, with his minute adherence to the letter of the law, misses the whole point of the case. Despite the fact that both Caponsacchi and Pompilia have testified that they were not lovers, Bottinius assumes that they were and expends considerable legal energy arguing that this liason does not matter. As he notes at the end, his oration "much exceeds in length / That famed Panegyric of Isocrates, / They say it took him fifteen years to pen" (9.1570–1573). In direct opposition to those orators who work spontaneously (who "put in just what rushed into [their] heads"), Bottinius proudly announces that he has to "prune and pare and print" (9.1574–1575). His pedantic attitude even affects how he takes his own physical pleasures. "I traverse Rome, feel thirsty," he posits; but he is incapable of simply buying a drink and satisfying his thirst. The legal impulse is too strong in him:

> [I] look for a wine-shop, find it by the bough
> Projecting as to say "Here wine is sold!"
> So much I know,—"sold:" but what sort of wine?
> Strong, weak, sweet, sour, home-made or foreign drink?
> . . . Exactly so, Law hangs her title forth. (9.1544–1551)

This sort of pedantry is the death of passion, of life; and it is exactly contrary to the animating love that prompts spontaneous action.

It is true that Guido claims to have acted instinctually, from impulse. The Pope imagines him thinking of himself as "a weak thing that gave way / To truth, to impulse only strong since true" (10.358–359), but the fact of the matter is that Guido rarely if ever acts spontaneously. He schemes, he plans; he has given over his whole life to the business of waiting on patrons, cooling his heels in dusty anterooms. His outburst of murderous anger is actually a function of a lifetime of repression and frustration. Guido himself recognizes this; to the representatives of the Church present with him in his condemned cell, he says,

> —blame yourselves
> For this eruption of the pent-up soul
> You prisoned first and played with afterward!
> "Deny myself" meant simply pleasure you,
> The sacred and superior, save the mark!
> You,—whose stupidity and insolence
> I must defer to, soothe at every turn,—
> Whose swine-like snuffling greed and grunting lust
> I had to wink at or help gratify—

> While the same passions,—dared they perk in me,
> Me, the immeasurably marked, by God,
> Master of the whole world of such as you,—
> I, boast such passions? 'Twas "Suppress them straight!"
> 　(11.1493–1505)

The whole moral scheme of *The Ring and the Book* tends away from the notion that "suppression is the word!" (11.1513).

If we consider this whole argument not from the point of view of the action, but from that of the text as a whole, the realm of interpretation, then we see a distinction between two sorts of hermeneutics. On the one hand, there is the pedant's approach to defining meaning (or "proof"), something that involves the careful definition of each term or word and necessarily runs into the deconstructionist *mise en abîme*, the infinite relativism of proliferating signifiers. But on the other hand is the Pope's approach, the approach of the true reader, defining meaning via the heart rather than the head, faith rather than reason, working through literature morally rather than scientifically. If *The Ring and the Book* does anything, it aligns Browning with moral faith rather than scientific reason; it is an epic of moral and aesthetic hermeneutics, and not (despite superficial appearances) a legal or scientific text.

Chapter Eight
The Long Poems of the 1870s

For the majority of critical studies of Browning, *The Ring and the Book* is the end, the great epic that (with *Sordello*) bookends the really significant work of Browning's writing life. Critics acknowledge that the great man went on writing, of course, but the consensus remains that the result was nothing but acres of barren verbiage. Of all the misrepresentations of Browning, this most enduring one is surely the least defensible. Far from stopping experimenting and engaging in poetry with *The Ring and the Book*, Browning went on to produce some of his most powerful and challenging work in his later life.

The neglect of the later Browning has produced some peculiar prejudices about the shape of his writing career. It is surprising to remember, for instance, that in the single decade of the 1870s Browning produced more work than he had managed in the 1830s, 1840s, and 1850s put together. Why Browning wrote so much is in itself an interesting question. I have already argued that the death of Elizabeth Barrett had freed up his facility with words; the scenario in which she wrote epics and he wrote short poems and spent his energies in supporting her had changed. By writing "Mr Sludge 'the Medium'" and by creating an epic to rival (indeed, surpass) *Aurora Leigh* out of material Elizabeth Barrett had found grisly and unappealing, Browning was in effect reacting against the dead hand of his wife's influence. The fact that he spent so much poetic energy attacking her sacred cows (particularly Napoleon III in *Prince Hohenstiel-Schwangau*) and defending objects of her scorn (in *Aristophanes Apology*) suggests the force of her influence. But the matter was not a straightforward working through of a process of bereavement; it was complicated by an event in Browning's life that was to have repercussions throughout the 1870s.

In 1869 Browning holidayed in Scotland. He was exhausted after the completion of the monumental masterpiece and worried about his son, Pen, who was showing signs of turning into a wastrel and an idler, and his grief for Elizabeth Barrett had been revived by writing the dedication to the "lyric Love" with which he began and ended *The Ring and the Book*. It seems that his emotions were in turmoil; it had been over eight years since Elizabeth's death, and his mind was turning toward his own emotional future, yet Elizabeth still loomed large in his life. While staying at the country seat of the beautiful, wealthy, and widowed Lady Ashburton, Browning proposed marriage. He had known Lady Ashburton for several years, and she was certainly eligible and desirable, if rather statuesque in her appearance and unpredictable in her moods. But Browning was in a psychological double bind. He wanted to marry Lady Ashburton, yet he had committed himself to Elizabeth Barrett forever; he hoped to find emotional balm in another marriage, but at the same time he felt that such a marriage would all but amount to bigamy. As a result, Browning proposed marriage in such a way as to almost certainly invite refusal. He asked for her hand but added that "[his] heart was buried in Florence" in Elizabeth Barrett's tomb and that, for him, "the attractiveness of a marriage with her lay in its advantage to Pen: two simple facts" (letter to Edith Story, April 4, 1872; in Hood, *Letters*, 170–171). These "facts" spurred Lady Ashburton into a furious rejection. Whether she might have accepted had Browning declared his *love* is a moot point, but declaring a simple matter of convenience was to be assured of rejection.

That Browning was bitterly wounded by this rejection is itself testament to the fact that he had invested more in the outcome, emotionally speaking, than he implied by saying, "I only want you as a mother for my son." What is undeniable is that for years afterwards Browning responded with uncharacteristic savageness when Lady Ashburton's name was so much as mentioned. "I see every now and then that contemptible Lady Ashburton," he wrote to a friend in 1874, "and mind her no more than any other black beetle—so long as it don't crawl up my sleeve" (letter to William Story, June 9, 1874; in Hood, *Letters*, 190). The figure of the femme fatale, the deadly and sadistic superior female, makes noteworthy appearances in his verse after this time. The nightmarish devil-woman in the lyric that concludes "Parleying with Daniel Bartoli" evidently owes a great deal to Browning's experience of Lady Ashbuton:

> Who bade you come, brisk-marching bold she-shape,
>> A terror with those black-balled worlds of eyes,
> That black hair bristling solid-built from nape
>> To crown it coils about? O dread surmise!
> Take, tread on, trample under past escape

Your capture, spoil and trophy! Do—devise
Insults for one who, fallen once, ne'er shall rise. (287–293)

If he felt trodden on and trampled by Lady Ashburton's rejection, he was also faced with the emotional difficulty of reconciling within himself his own apparent rejection of an eternal bond of love with Elizabeth Barrett. His problem was compounded of the need to emotionally and intellectually reconcile his desire to escape from her influence with his desire to reunite with her, to reconnect after the grave. Unsurprisingly, then, the theme of infidelity, which had provided him with so much material over the years, was to take on a more literalized appearance in the 1870s. Women of various sorts and with various (but usually overwhelming) effects on men populate the 1870s poems as never before. The chief psychic equation (as it were) from which the later poetry emerges seems to be an opposition between Elizabeth Barrett and representations of Lady Ashburton, between wife and seductive other, between duty and sexuality.

One aspect of this opposition is geographical. The poetry of *Men and Women* and *The Ring and the Book* had been Italian with a capital *I*, in terms of not just location and scenery but all the minute detail and verisimilitude of lived experience. One of the many rings in *The Ring and the Book* is the two-way link that Elizabeth Barrett had forged between England and Italy with her own Italian poems. The poem ends with a reassertion of that link, praising the Italian poet Nicolo Tommasei and hymning "Lyric Love / Thy rare gold ring of verse (the poet praised) / Linking our England to his Italy!" (868–870). But apart from a few shorter poems in *Pacchiarotto and How He Worked in Distemper* (1876), Browning set none of his 1870s poems in Italy. Whereas in the 1850s and 1860s the dominant country in Browning's imagination was Italy, in the 1870s that place was taken by two rather different nations: France and Greece.

Browning stayed in France often during the 1870s, even electing to visit in 1870 when the country was losing the Franco-Prussian war and being invaded by German soldiers—an odd holiday destination, we might think. He spoke and read French fluently and felt at home among French people. Moreover, France served almost as an embodiment of a poetic ideal. France for Browning was a woman, so French topics, settings, and manners enabled him to explore his own relationship to womankind. In *Prince Hohenstiel-Schwangau* (1871) the narrator, a thinly disguised Napoleon III, talks about being emperor in terms of his "mistress," the French Assembly, and by extension "La France" herself, who "chose this man" as president "to serve her" (1234–1235). In *Fifine at the Fair* (1872) Browning casts his Don Juan (traditionally a Spaniard) as a Frenchman and has him narrate his very French debate about questions of sexual infidelity between his wife, Elvire, and the seductive gypsy, Fifine. Similarly, *Red Cotton Night-Cap Country* (1873) is set in France and elaborates the (true) story of a French man obsessed with a beautiful woman; he is so torn between his desire for her and the strictures of respectable society that he is driven to suicide. The meditative *La Saisiaz* (1878) is set in French Switzerland, and the jollier *The Two Poets of Croisic* (1878) in Brittany.

Greece had been the early love of Browning's life, as the calmly beautiful "Artemis Prologuizes" (1841) attests, before Elizabeth Barrett had decreed that "Christianity is itself a worthy myth and poetically acceptable" and that Greek mythology was no longer relevant for poetry. It is easy to see the remarkable outpouring of Greek poems of the 1870s as another symptom of Browning's sense of artistic freedom from his dead wife's influence. *Balaustion's Adventure* (1871), *Aristophanes' Apology* (1875), his translation of three Attic tragedies (the *Agamemnon* of Aeschylus [1877] and Euripides' *Alkestis* [which appears in *Balaustion's Adventure*] and *Herakles* [in *Aristophanes' Apology*]), and numerous mythic allusions in the French poems (particularly in *Fifine*) as well as in shorter works ("Numpholeptos" in 1876, "Pheidippides" in 1879, "Pan and Luna" in 1880) are a testament to Browning's immersion in Greek literature and culture. If France functioned for him as representative of ideal womanhood and certain physical pleasures (wine, food, sex), then Greece stood for another contradictory doubling: on the one hand a close-textured intellectualism; on the other a profound Dionysiac irrationalism. In particular, *Aristophanes' Apology* and *The Agamemnon of Aeschylus* blend these two elements in a heady mixture, although Browning's first major "Greek" poem has often been seen as rather banal.

I. *Balaustion's Adventure* (1871)

Elizabeth Barrett's presence hovers over *Balaustion's Adventure*. Partly this is because the story of Alkestis (the dead wife, the grieving husband) has certain obvious resonances with Browning's own personal life, but it is also because Elizabeth Barrett is specifically invoked in the text. The name "Balaustion" actually means "wild pomegranate flower," recalling the first contact between Elizabeth and Robert, when she had made praising reference to him ("some 'Pomegranate' . . . within blood-tinctured"). "Ba" was Browning's pet name for his wife, and the epigraph to the work is from Elizabeth's "Wine of Cyprus," a text referred to again in line 2671.

> Our Euripides, the human
> > With his droppings of warm tears,
> And his touches of things common
> > Till they rose to touch the spheres.

"Our Euripides," with its Anglo-Hellenic pun ("Our-Your"), suggests universality, the "warm tears" suggesting perhaps sentimentality. Both are present in *Balaustion's Adventure*. It is worth noting that the scatologically-minded Swinburne found inadvertent humor in the notion of Euripides' "droppings," and his letters contain several cackling references to the implications of the phrase. If in *Balaustion's Adventure* Browning is too misty-eyed at the memory of his wife to recognize such low comedy, at least *Aristophanes' Apology* rights the balance.

The earlier poem is, as its dedication attests, "a May-month amusement," a relative lightweight in the Browning canon. We are introduced to Balaustion, a beautiful Rhodian girl, at the time of the Peloponnesian war. The Athenian fleet has been defeated at Syracuse, and Balaustion and others take flight on a ship at Kaunus, a seaport that belongs to Rhodes. They come across and are pursued by a pirate ship, but Balaustion gives heart to the rowers by singing an Aeschylean song that had been sung at the battle of Salamis. The ship arrives at Syracuse and asks for shelter, but the Syracusans refuse the request on the grounds that they are at war with Athens. When the people on the ship insist that they are Karians, subjects of Rhodes, they receive the reply that "all Athens echoed in that song from Aeschylus which was ringing over the sea." Things seems hopeless—it looks as though the ship will be turned away to face doom at the hands of the pirates—when somebody on shore cries out, "wait—do they know any verses from Euripides?"

Balaustion not only loves and knows Euripides, but has the necessary narrative gifts to be able to recreate the experience of attending a performance of a Euripides play. The Rhodians are brought ashore to the temple of Herakles, and on the temple steps Balaustion recites the story of Euripides' play *Alkestis*, half repeating Euripides' words, half describing a performance she has seen "at Kameiros this very year." The bulk of

Balaustion's Adventure is taken up with this retelling of *Alkestis*—how Admetus is doomed to die young unless somebody is prepared to take his place, how nobody is prepared to make the sacrifice except his loving wife, Alkestis, and how she then dies, to be finally rescued from the underworld by Herakles himself as a return for Admetus's selfless hospitality. The recital delights the Syracusans, who accept the Rhodians to their hearts.

The work seems to be advancing a simple moral about the power of poetry to materially affect the world, a moral underlined at various points: "Greeks are Greeks, and hearts are hearts, / And poetry is power . . ." (235–236); "What's poetry except a power that makes? / And, speaking to one sense, inspires the rest, / Pressing them all into its service?" (318–320). But a "critic and whippersnapper" in Balaustion's audience, objecting to her technique, raises another, more fundamental issue. The whippersnapper does not like Balaustion's version of the play because "the girl departs from truth!" (308): she describes facial expressions even though Greek actors wore masks and adumbrates the text with various descriptive passages that are not present in the original. The issue concerns fidelity to Euripides' actual text. As far as Browning is concerned, the whippersnapper is wrong because true poetry is not about a slavish attention to minute particulars but about the vital recreation of imaginative energy. It is not about the dry pedantries of Dominus Hyacinthus de Archangelis or Juris Doctor Johannes-Baptista Bottinius but about the spontaneity and imaginative courage of Caponsacchi or the Pope. But there is a profusion of specific biographical reference in *Balaustion's Adventure*, including the unavoidable identification of Balaustion with Elizabeth Barrett, of the "critic and whippersnapper" with Alfred Austin (a critic of small stature who had violently attacked Browning in the 1860s and 1870s), and even of a member of Balaustion's audience with Robert Browning—"one man" of whom Balaustion announces, "we are to marry" (265–274). What this means is that the question of fidelity involves more than aesthetics. In particular, *Balaustion's Adventure* is a poem about marriage. A marriage occurs in the frame story, when Balaustion and her lover wed, and a marriage is broken in *Alkestis*, when Admetos's wife dies to save him, and then revivified when Herakles conquers Death. Poetry, indeed, is represented as a sort of marriage: Euripides' original and Balaustion's imagination join together to produce *Balaustion's Adventure*. Death itself is represented not as an end but as a rite of passage that leads to a more intimate and loving marriage. Alkestis, returned from the underworld by

Herakles, is compared to Persephone, but in a way that hints at a buried erotic subtext:

> Whereat the softened eyes
> Of the lost maidenhood that lingered still
> Straying among the flowers in Sicily . . .
> . . . broke through humanity
> Into the orbed splendour of a God. (2623–2628)

Browning was artistically reworking his marriage, turning death into nothing but a maidenhead that all married couples must eventually lose. This work constitutes a reaffirmation of his fidelity to the memory of his dead wife.

II. *Prince Hohenstiel-Schwangau* (1871)

Browning's next work, however, saw him virulently attack one of his wife's old heroes. Napoleon III, emperor since 1851, had in 1870 led the French into a disastrous war against the Prussians. On defeat he had fled to England, where he lived out the remainder of his days. Browning's poem seems ("seems" because we later discover it is actually a dream vision) to be set after his fall, with Napoleon visiting a rather run-down prostitute in a room off Leicester Square; he addresses himself to this woman ("You have seen better days, dear? So have I") and proceeds to give her his life story, although as always with Browning the "reveal-ment of myself" (22) is less concerned with the external actions and more with the labyrinthine windings of the narrator's character.

It is again a poem about fidelity, although in this instance the rela-tionship is not that of husband and wife but that of the poem's Prince and the idealized female country he rules. The Prince's problem is that it appears he has betrayed his trust as ruler, has been effectively unfaithful to his people. He defends himself on a variety of grounds, notably that political expediency dictates a politician's actions. The kingdom of Hohenstiel-Schwangau (i.e., France) chooses her "man," her "President"; but the president discovers that his mistress's servants did not "mean to keep faith" (1248). The Prince represents himself as a man battling against all the odds, trying to keep the kingdom on an even keel. But with the Faustian echo of a chiming clock bringing the reverie to an end ("One,— / Two, three, four, five,—yes, five the *pendule* warns!" [2073]), the Prince awakens to discover that it had all been a dream, that he has not yet fallen from power. His self-justifications, which had served "well enough / I' the darkness," when brought to the light "are found, like those famed cave-fish, to lack eye / And organ for the upper magnitude" (2106–2109). Where he had been characterizing himself as the faithful husband of his country, he now acknowledges his weakness for "the lust o' the flesh, lust of the eye, / And pride of life" (2118–2119). The politician, it seems, no matter how noble his aim, cannot keep faith in the political arena. Lies follow, even if the aim is truth. "Alack," the Prince notes at the end of his monologue, "one lies oneself / Even in the stating that one's end was truth" (2123–2124). Sordello had made a similar discovery; the political arena corrodes personal integrity.

It is interesting to compare Browning with another great midcentury writer who worked over much of the same ground. Karl Marx had examined the phenomenom of Napoleon III in *The Eighteenth Brumaire of Louis Napoleon* (1852). Almost certainly Browning did not read Marx's work. Despite the fact that both thinkers espoused political opinions that were (to one degree or another) left of center, their views seem to be diametrically positioned. The critical consensus has been that Browning is interested in the personal, Marx in the political. More specifically, Marx sees the personal as political, whereas Browning, in *Schwangau* certainly, sees the political as personal. Browning is often lauded as a poet of great psychological acuity, rarely if ever as a poet of great political insight (as if the two arenas were entirely distinct). *Prince Hohenstiel-Schwangau* is often described as a text without political sophistication, as an attempt to see the historical and political entirely in personal terms. "Neither Browning nor his wife," suggests Robert Pearsall, "had developed clear ideas of the historical forces that lie behind politics. In particular, Elizabeth Barrett envisioned political processes as romantic exercises in good or evil, and the dead hand of Elizabeth Barrett is easily visible in *Prince Hohenstiel-Schwangau*." Clyde de L. Ryals thinks more highly of the poem but nevertheless insists that it is "more psychological than political." Other critics agree—the poem "fails" because the author "knew and cared so little about economics and government."[1]

There have been few Marxist studies of Browning.[2] Yet Browning deserves credit for anatomizing if not exactly history, then certainly a particular ideology—a bourgeois ideology of which *Schwangau* is a trenchant political critique. It is true Browning's first artistic impulse was personal, but that should not distract us from the fact that his interests were also political. By *political* I do not mean the plodding (and to my mind curiously inchoate) party affiliation of the sonnet "Why I Am a Liberal" so much as an awareness of the way social environment determines individual being. A statement from Marx can provide a gloss for Browning's monologues in general: his poems articulate the view that "all social life is essentially practical. All the mysteries which lead theory into mysticism find their rational solution in human practice and in the comprehension of this practice."[3] In *The Eighteenth Brumaire* Marx set out to analyze a certain bourgeois mind-set embodied, even apotheosized, in Napoleon III. Browning set out in *Prince Hohenstiel-Schwangau* to do precisely the same thing.

III. *Fifine at the Fair* (1872)

Roma King has called *Fifine at the Fair* "one of the four poems essential to an understanding of Browning," the other three being *Sordello*, *The Ring and the Book*, and the *Parleyings*.[4] It certainly presents as massive a challenge as these three other key works. On the surface, *Fifine* seems to be a look inside the mind of that figure from erotic myth, Don Juan; in 2350 rolling alexandrine couplets, the old seducer talks to his wife, Elvire, about his sexual passion for a gypsy girl, Fifine, whom they encountered earlier in the day at a Pornic fair. Indeed, the subject is unusually frank for a mid-Victorian poem, and it was probably only its obscurity that saved the work from scandal.

Fifine is one of the most resolutely binary poems of Browning's oeuvre: Don Juan sees everything, most especially women, in terms of oppositions. His is a sensibility that can only relate to women by pigeonholing them as either madonnas or whores. The first type of womankind (as Don Juan would see it) is represented by Elvire, his wife: she is pale, a "daisy meek, or maiden violet" (197), whereas Fifine is dark and sensual, a "dusk-leaved rose" (157). Elvire is put on a pedestal by the narrator:

> —the rose it is, I wot
> Only the rose we pluck and place, unwronged a jot,
> No worse for homage done by every devotee,
> I' the proper loyal throne . . .
> We gather daisy meek, or maiden violet:
> I think it is Elvire we love, and not Fifine. (190–198)

"Think" (not "know"), of course, is significant: when the gypsy Fifine is introduced into the poem, the narrator speaks with far greater vitality and energy. Working dynamically against this rather static and distant representation of the violet-like Elvire is the brown vigor of Fifine's sensuousness in her page-boy's costume:

> with breasts'-birth commence
> The boy, and page-costume, till pink and impudence
> End admirably all; complete the creature trips
> Our way now, brings sunshine upon her spangled hips,
> As here she fronts us full, with pose half-frank, half-fierce!
> (164–168)

Fifine stands for a freedom, although a dangerous freedom; Elvire is safety, but also restriction. This fundamental distinction reflects itself even in the mechanics of the verse (for instance, section XVIII of the poem, which discusses Elvire, is entirely end-stopped; in section XX, where Fifine is introduced, the end-stopping breaks down and the verse becomes markedly freer).

This binary opposition is articulated via a number of thematic pairings. In fact, the poem contrasts a great many things—freedom/constraint, truth/lies, flesh/spirit, sex/pure love, and so on—in much the same manner as *The Ring and the Book*. The poem drives home the contrasts Don Juan sees between Elvire and Fifine with continually reiterated images of opposition. Elvire is white to the point of transparency ("How pallidly you pause / . . . so white! . . . / suppose you are a ghost?" [2306–2310]), whereas Fifine is dark and solid ("swarth / . . . a dusk-leaved rose carved from a cocoa-nut" [151–157]). Utilizing the metaphor of woman-as-ship, the narrator describes Elvire as a solid merchant ship becalmed, Fifine as a small rapid skiff:

> And good Elvire is moored, with not a breath to flap
> The yards of her, no life or ripple to o'erlap
> Keel, much less, prow. What care? Since here's a cockle shell,
> Fifine, that's taut and crank, and carries just as well. (1302–1305)

In broader terms, "Elvire is land not sea— / The solid land, the safe" (2314–2315) and Fifine the sea, "Fifine, the foam flake." (2299) Of course, it really goes without saying that such objectification of women is a tactic of oppression. As Isobel Armstrong points out with reference to this poem, "Don Juan is an intelligent, corrupt poet" who "polarizes women into whore and virtuous matron because this sexual dualism makes possible a subtle denigration of both women."[5]

With such rigidly demarcated polarities it might seem that there is no way for a synthesis, for the sort of coming together that characterizes *The Ring and the Book*. In fact, Don Juan does grope toward a way out of his own selfishness. The key word is "share," and about halfway through the poem the narrator seems to recognize that his own male self-indulgence is cause for concern:

> both share
> The chemic secret, learn—where I lit force, why there
> You drew forth lambent pity,—where I found only food
> For self-indulgence. (889–892)

This is expressed in terms of chromatics—the metaphor turns on the way the colors of the rainbow can be mixed ("blent") together to make white:

> changing each as changed, till, wholly blent,
> Our old things shall be new, and, what we both ignite,
> Fuse, lose the varicolour in achromatic white! (895–897)

The situation is summed up in a line from Aeschylus that Don Juan quotes several times in its original Greek: *Theosutos e broteios eper kekramene*—"God, mortal, or both together mixed." It is this blending, this kekramity, that emerges as the poem's moral perspective: instead of women being forced into opposing stereotypes, they should be viewed as complex combinations. To do otherwise not only promotes infidelity (Don Juan creeps off at the end of the poem to try and find sexual satisfaction with Fifine), but also ignores truth. Don Juan almost makes this last point when he puts society in the dock for creating people where

> Each has a false outside, whereby a truth is forced
> To issue from within: truth, falsehood, are divorced
> By the excepted eye . . . (1505–1507)

The "great clearing up" can only come when we realize that the world is morally "parti-coloured" (1511). Don Juan, though, does not follow his argument through to its logical conclusion: when he quotes *Theosutos e broteios eper kekramene* a second time (2210), it is not to espouse a doctrine of synthesis, but to subvert it; he translates it and the whole Aeschylean passage it comes from into comically bathetic English. He is not equal to the moral. As he himself admits, "I dwindle at the close, / Down to mere commonplace" (2228–2229).

As is, perhaps, appropriate to a poem that charts the inability to progress to a synthesis from thesis and antithesis, the underlying shape and rhythm of *Fifine at the Fair* is circular. Just as Don Juan's argument circles fruitlessly, returning in the end without having at all altered his reprobate behavior, so the poem itself follows a circular path. It begins with Don Juan and Fifine walking to the fair; it ends with them walking back. Don Juan makes the point explicit when he talks of walking the "last little mile that makes the circuit just," adding, "we end where we began; that consequence is clear" (2241–2242). Don Juan's repetition of certain key phrases also stresses circularity—for instance, "trip and skip, link arm in arm with me, / Like husband and like wife" (1–2, 1519–1520) and, as has already been noted, *Theosutos e broteios eper kekramene*. The last couplet of the epilogue even has the same rhyme as the first couplet of the poem proper ("She" / "me!"). Don Juan claims to be returning to the solidity of his wife:

> no matter how it range
> From Helen to Fifie, Elvire brings back the change
> To permanence. Here, too, loves ends where love began.
> (2284–2286)

He is characterizing himself as being someone that toyed with the idea of infidelity, but returned eventually to the faithfulness of Elvire. In fact, his monologue explores and almost achieves a method of avoiding infidelity by coming to terms with the reality of womankind, but it is thwarted from doing so in the end by Don Juan's own habits of lust— the actual trajectory of the poem is inverse to the one claimed by the narrator. Don Juan is clearly a flawed character and deliberately represented as such, yet the poem is not a wholly negative undertaking. Browning shows us both the answer to Don Juan's dilemma and Don Juan's inability to avail himself of it. Browning's view of the possibilities of life remains optimistic, even if his commentary on the character of his protagonist is not.

IV. *Red Cotton Night-Cap Country* (1873)

The twin elements of France and marriage crop up again in *Red Cotton Night-Cap Country*. Like *The Ring and the Book*, it is a bizarre, grisly, and true tale in which violence and death result indirectly from society's stifling marriage conventions. In this case, the problem is that the protagonist, the rich and highly strung jeweler Leonce Miranda, falls in love with an already married woman, the beautiful Clara. Clara's marriage is emotionally over, but the fact that technically she has a husband means that Miranda and Clara cannot marry and have to live together beyond the pale of society. When Miranda's mother sternly objects to this immorality, the guilt-stricken fellow attempts suicide. After the failure of this attempt, he returns to Clara. When his mother dies, Miranda believes that his cohabitation with Clara had driven her to her grave; his guilt reasserts itself. In a striking scene, having sworn to abjure his lover, he burns her letters in an open fire. He thrusts the whole lot into the fire—letters, the box they came in, and his own hands—

> Into the burning grate and held them there
> "Burn, burn and purify my past!" said he,
> Calmly, as if he felt no pain at all. (2589–2591)

This self-mutilation might be thought appropriate punishment by a self-condemned jeweler, who is after all a worker with his hands. The situation where a man is torn between the demands of a dead woman for spiritual purity and the company of a sensual, loving, and living woman, is familiar enough in the Browning canon post-Elizabeth Barrett. Miranda goes back to Clara, loving her too much to stay away; and when he leaps to his death from the top of one of his country mansion's towers, it is tempting to see the action as another neurotic suicide attempt, one that this time succeeds. But Browning's insistence that Miranda acted rationally, according to his own beliefs—he hoped that God would take that moment to effect a miracle and fly him through the air to a nearby church—suggests that Browning was deeply involved in the sort of emotional dilemma Miranda found himself in. In essence Miranda's position is summed up by the poem's subtitle, "Turf and Towers," in which the turf represents the earth (including physical pleasures and desires) and the towers stand for spiritual aspiration. It is a similar distinction to that between sky and water in *Fifine*, the main difference being that if you jump fifty feet into the sea, you are likely to survive, unlike Miranda, who ends lying "stone dead . . . on the turf" (3594).

V. *Aristophanes' Apology* (1875)

The sequel to *Balaustion's Adventure*—the third longest of Browning's works (after *The Ring and the Book* and *Sordello*)—is complex, intellectual, and lengthy where the prequel is straightforward, sentimental, and short. Indeed, *Aristophanes' Apology* is so lengthy and complex that it has been almost wholly neglected by critics. For most, it represents nothing more than an example of intimidatingly erudite and hopelessly esoteric argumentation. A summary of the poem does not make it sound inviting. The narrative is set after the final defeat and downfall of Athens, at the end of the Peloponnesian war (at the close of the fifth century B.C.). Balaustion, married to her admirer (who, we are now told, is called "Euthukles"), is sailing from the destroyed city to her home on Rhodes. On board this ship she speaks the vast length of the monologue that is *Aristophanes' Apology*, taking us back to the day she and her husband heard that Euripides was dead. As the two of them prepare to honor the memory of the tragedian, they are interrupted by the comic dramatist Aristophanes bursting into their home. Balaustion and Aristophanes then engage in a lengthy debate, or argument, over the respective merits of tragedy and comedy, Euripides and Aristophanes. Balaustion crowns her defence of Euripides with a recital of his last play, *Herakles*. Aristophanes concedes that Euripides was indeed a marvelous writer, recites a fragmentary lyric of his own, and leaves in good humor. The poem ends with Balaustion recalling the destruction of Athens by the Spartans and looking forward to her happily married life with Euthukles on Rhodes.

Aristophanic comedy was chiefly a vitriolic and scatological satire on contemporary figures; sex and toilet-humor played a large part. To Balaustion this is merely disgusting; she talks of one of Aristophanes' plays, *Lysistrata*, as a "pustule" and asks the waves "said to wash pollution from the world" to "take that plague-memory" (47–48). The subject of *Lysistrata*, incidentally, is a women-organized sex strike; wives vow to deny their husbands conjugal rights until the men stop fighting a stupid and senseless war. Balaustion, who seemed so fresh and adventurous in *Balaustion's Adventure*, seems to have become something of an old prude. Aristophanes attacks Euripides on the same grounds, interestingly, as those that Balaustion uses to attack him; which is to say, Aristophanes accuses Euripides of degrading tragedy, bringing in common people and vulgar speech (2114f.), challenging the old values, denying the existence of the gods, and so forth. In more general terms, he sees Euripides' plays as cold and antilife, whereas he asserts his own ribaldry as warm and vital.

> "Unworld the world!" frowns he, my opposite.
> I cry "Life!" "Death," he groans, "our better Life!"
> Despise what is—the good and graspable,
> Prefer the out of sight and in at mind,
> To village-joy, the well-side violet patch,
> The jolly club-feast when our field's in soak,
> Roast thrushes, haresoup, peasoup, deep washed down
> With Peparethian [a wine]; the prompt paying off
> That black-eyed, brown-skinned, country-flavoured wench
> We caught among our brushwood foraging:
> On these look fig-juice, curdle up life's cream,
> And fall to magnifying misery! (1947–1958)

Balaustion might object that Aristophanes' position here reduces the wonder and spiritual richness of life to good food, wine, and sex; but it is easy to come away from *Aristophanes' Apology* with the sense that Aristophanes has by far the more attractive argument. Balaustion's narrow adherence to somebody else's art versus Aristophanes' own fecund and potent creativity; the rather weak verse of her speeches versus the muscular and thumping coarseness of his (as instanced above); above all her piety versus his zest for living—these contrasts set up the whole enterprise in the manner of a head-to-head between Andrea del Sarto on the one hand and Fra Lippo Lippi on the other. Aristophanes also has by far the bulk of the text, if we don't count the transcription of *Herakles* as part of Balaustion's argument.

As Daniel Karlin points out, if *Aristophanes' Apology* were actually about the relative literary merits of two long-dead Greek playwrights, it would indeed be as tedious and esoteric as its enemies have suggested.[6]

But it is not really about such recondite things. In fact, Browning is working through his two chief influences. Euripides exerts a pull from beyond the grave, exhorting him to purity, seriousness, and religion (Balaustion insists that Euripides' doubts about the Olympian gods are simply a reflection of the fact that he has progressed beyond paganism toward a monotheism, a sort of Christianity *avant la lettre*). Aristophanes praises life and enjoyment, the full enjoyment of the here-and-now. He says he simply can't help flinging mud at the idiots who surround him. Balaustion considers it undignified, but Aristophanes joyfully announces, "would not I rub each face in its own filth[?]" Balaustion may declare that her "heart burned up" in indignation at the thought of such a credo, but Browning himself followed Aristophanes' advice. Attacked in the press by the pint-sized Alfred Austin, Browning responded with Aristophanic vigor (if not quite Aristophanic obscenity) in *Pacchiarotto and How He Worked in Distemper* (1876), in which he lambasts Austin as a "Quilp-Hop-o'-my-thumb," a "Banjo-Byron" (Austin was also a poet, not a terribly good one), and a "homunculus" before he reins himself in with a footnote: ("Who would be satirical / On a thing so very small?" 520–534). Austin also crops up in *Aristophanes' Apology*, under the pseudonym "Dogface Eruxis, the small satirist," a "manikin" who "butted at my knee" (1673–1675). Aristophanes would have no qualms about hurling shit at such a figure, even though in the process he may become "immortally immerded" (1670); Balaustion, and Elizabeth Barrett, would not agree.

On the surface it might seem, however, that Browning identifies himself with the embodiment of his dead wife, with the Euripides who was in his own day a radical and experimental writer and who was criticized by figures of conservative literary opinion—a writer such as, we might think, Browning was in the nineteenth century. Yet the figure who sounds most like Browning as the play goes on is Aristophanes, not Euripides; and the final irony of the piece may be the translation of *Herakles* that occupies a central place in the poem's construction (3535–5084). Balaustion defends Euripides as the arch-rationalist, the soul who strove "to teach and bless" the world (502):

> Speak to the infinite intelligence,
> Sing to the everlasting sympathy! (219–220)

But *Herakles* is anything but rational. It begins straightforwardly enough with Herakles' return from the underworld, just as in *Alkestis*.

He finds his children in danger and rescues them; but then, in a startling and unprepared-for development, the embodiment of madness descends and renders Herakles insane. Mad Herakles kills all his children, thinking them deer and himself a hunter. The play ends with Herakles regaining his sanity and realizing what he has done; Theseus appears and promises to take him to Athens to atone for his crimes. In other words, *Herakles* is a violent exploration of the *ir*rational, the chaotic, and the violent.

Moreover, it is translated with the peculiar, unidiomatic literalism that Browning brought to all his translations from the tragedians. The most famous example is his rendering of Aeschylus's *Agamemnon* (1877), a translation that he boasted (in the preface) was "literal at every cost save that of absolute violence to the language." But critics detected just such violence in Browning's treatment of Aeschylus's difficult play; a Browningesque delight in difficult syntax, clogging consonants, and awkward rhythm. And violence is present in his *Herakles*, too, not just in the extremes of the plot but in the very style of Browning's translation itself. And this is the violence we find mirrored in the speech of Aristophanes (a man who delights in "pulverizing" pygmies and "flogg[ing] while skin could purple and flesh start" [1654, 1659]) rather than in the placidity of Balaustion.

VI. *The Inn Album* (1875)

Based once again on a true story, *The Inn Album* is also yet another story about a man's choice between two women, one offered to him for sexual reasons, the other young and pure. It is the familiar Browningesque equation, although here given a new twist. An old rake and a young blade have been playing cards all night, and thanks to the vicissitudes of luck the older man now owes the younger 10,000 pounds. In lieu of payment the older man offers the younger man one of his cast-off mistresses, a woman he had seduced when she was young and in love with him, who after being discarded had gone off to live a quiet life with an unsuspecting vicar as a husband. It so happens that the younger man has feelings for the older woman, although he is engaged to be married to a young woman; coincidentally, the two women have come to the inn where the two men have been gaming all night. The older man blackmails the older woman by threatening to reveal all to her husband. Rather than submit, the woman takes poison, but before dying reveals the older man's villainy to the younger man. The young man flies at the throat of the villain and kills him. The scene ends with the innocent young woman about to enter and discover this grisly scene of death.

Critics have generally seen this work as an English manifestation of the new continental Realism, embodied most famously in the novels of Balzac and Zola. One difference is that Browning, after the intellectual expansiveness of *Aristophanes' Apology*, here returned to a more elliptical, allusive, and compacted style—a more Browningesque style, we might say. Henry James, reviewing the work for the *Nation*, shook his head sagely and saw only incomprehensible "hieroglyphics and symbols." "*The Inn Album* reads like a series of rough notes for a poem," he observed. More modern critics have seen more merit in the piece. Clyde Ryals is certain that "it is the formal experimentation" that makes the work "significant among Browning's works. Quite unlike anything he had attempted earlier, it combines melodrama with the narrative technique of the novel."[7]

Formally interesting it certainly is, yet one of the striking things about *The Inn Album* is the way it makes complex mental processes appear clear, while at the same time making simple narrative seem obscure. There is remarkably little action in the 3,000 lines of text, but when events do move along, comprehension of the narrative is obstructed by an obliqueness that is all the more remarkable for being suddenly introduced. The dying speech of the older woman, for instance, is quite clearly stated. She speaks bitterly of the older man, assures the younger man that she never suspected him of being part of the other's villainy ("I did well, trusting instinct: knew your hand / Had never joined with his in fellowship / Over this pact of infamy" [2997–2999]). Events are clearly coming to a head—but when they arrive the reader is liable simply to be baffled.

> "So!"

> A tiger-flash—yell, spring, and scream: halloo!
> Death's out and on him, has and holds him—ugh!
> But *ne trucidet coram populo*
> *Juvenis senem*! Right the Horatian rule!

> There, see how soon a quiet comes to pass!
> (3015–3019)

What exactly has happened? Who does what, and to whom? Even if we are well educated enough to recognize the Latin quotation—"Do not show the youngster killing the old man in front of the audience," which is a variation of Horace's instruction in *The Art of Poetry* "Do not show Medea killing her children in front of the audience"—and if we therefore realize that the young man has strangled the old, it is still not possible to entirely untangle the lines. What exactly is the "tiger-flash"? Who says, "ugh"? The old man? The young? The narrator?

The point is that instead of smoothly revealing the narrative denouement, Browning chooses precisely this moment to snarl things up, to throw some Latin sand in his reader's eye, to hold up the progress of the piece. Determining who is referred to by the "him" in line 3017 means interpreting the Latin, which is not only phrased in such a way as to hold off this interpretation for one line (3018: "But do not show before the audience the killing of . . .") but also requires the reader's being able to distinguish the accusative from the dative case in the next line (is it "the young by the old"? Or "the old by the young"?). Published without notes of any kind, the poem has an awkward way of revealing the climax. Besides, the Horation scruple seems oddly out of place in a poem that has already dealt unashamedly with all manner of immorality, sexual and other.

Chapter Nine

Short Poetry of the 1870s and 1880s

Browning spent a decade writing seven long poems, from *The Ring and the Book* to *The Inn Album*, and the critics had been negative throughout most of the 1870s; not unreasonably, his first collection to include short poetry since *Dramatis Personae* was almost wholly concerned with the poet's relationship with his audience. The title poem of *Pacchiarotto and How He Worked in Distemper* (1876) attacks Browning's most pertinacious critic, Alfred Austin, by remembering a long-dead Siennese painter of diminutive size who savaged everybody and everything and was eventually driven off and forced to hide in a grave with a rotting corpse. Less vitriolic are poems such as "At the Mermaid," in which Shakespeare is given voice to dismiss those who cannot distinguish between Shakespeare's creations and his private life. "Here's my work," he says; "does work discover — / What was rest from work—my life?" (17–18). The answer is no, the poet's "work" does not give insights into his "life," nor should it. Indeed, *Pacchiarotto* finds Browning rather testy on the subject of his privacy.

"House" is a direct assertion of the sanctity of the author's private life. It takes as its text a line from Wordsworth's poem "Scorn Not the Sonnet." Wordsworth praises Shakespeare's sonnets because they, unlike the plays, reveal the inner life of the writer: "With this key / Shakespeare unlocked his heart." It is a line Browning cites twice in his poem, twice misquoting it as if to show his disdain for the sentiment.

> Shall I sonnet-sing you about myself?
>> Do I live in a house you would like to see?
> Is it scant of gear, has it store of pelf?
>> "Unlock my heart with a sonnet-key?" (1–4)

Browning resents the intrusion and likens it to a house broken open by an earthquake into which passersby may poke their noses. He imagines what ordinary folk see when they peer into the private life of the writer:

> "Odd tables and chairs for a man of wealth!
> What a parcel of musty old books about!
> He smoked—no wonder he lost his health!
>
> "I doubt if he bathed before he dressed.
> A brasier?—the pagan, he burned perfumes!
> You see it is proved, what the neighbours guessed:
> His wife and himself had separate rooms." (22–28)

Browning is deliberately, we might say almost heavy-handedly, distancing himself from the subject of even this imagined intrusion. He did not smoke, he made a point of bathing regularly, and he did not burn perfumes. Another perspective, and a common one among critics, is that Browning is actually making a point about Dante Gabriel Rossetti and his recently published collection of sonnets, *The House of Life* (the first installment of which had appeared in 1870). The transgression signified by Rossetti's work did not have to do, of course, with strange furniture, musty books, or even incense burning, but with hints of the sexual life ("His wife and himself had separate rooms"). Browning objects to sexually explicit material not so much on the grounds of its depraving effect as on the grounds of privacy. Could Shakespeare have transgressed so?

> "Hoity toity! A street to explore,
> Your house the exception! 'With this same key
> Shakespeare unlocked his heart,' once more!"
> Did Shakespeare? If so, the less Shakespeare he! (37–40)

We can read the last line as "insofar as he laid bare his private feelings, Shakespeare was acting uncharacteristically." Equally likely is the reading "if our greatest poet did such a thing, then he forfeits some of his claim to our respect."

"Shop," also in *Pacchiarotto*, explores similar territory; this time it is a shopkeeper whose house/shop is open to any and all manner of people. "Fears and Scruples" explores the same issue from the other side of the fence, as it were. The relationship here is between Browning as reader and Shelley as poet: the narrator of the poem feels that once upon a time he truly loved an unnamed "unseen friend"; something, however, has intervened and destroyed how he originally felt about the person (Browning's discovery of Shelley's irregular sex life had deeply shocked him). But did the narrator ever really know his man? "Pleasant fancy! for I had but letters, / Only knew of actions by heresay" (9–10). The poem ends with the same rhetoric as "House," with an interlocutor wondering why the narrator did not know the person better:

> "Had his house no window? At first nod,
>
> > Would you not have hailed him?" Hush, I pray you!
>
> What if this friend happen to be—God? (46–9)

In other words, the narrator's knowledge of this person is similar to mankind's knowledge of God, which is to say partial and founded upon certain documents which may or may not be authentic (Browning's "Essay on Shelley" had originally been an introduction to a collection of Shelley's letters, until it was discovered that the letters were forgeries). Seeing the case from both sides shows how complex a matter it is, how impossible it is to ground knowledge in epistemological certainty, and how understanding must therefore be based on faith and love.

The two volumes of *Dramatic Idyls* (*First Series*, 1879; *Second Series*, 1880) marked a return to territory more familiar to Browning's rapidly increasing audience. Despite the huge and frequently off-putting output of the 1870s, Browning's reputation was higher than ever. In 1881, indeed, Browning's friend F. J. Furnivall set up a Browning Society "to learn more of the meaning of the poet's utterances; and then . . . bring others under the same influence that has benefited himself." There were already societies founded in honor of Wordsworth and Shelley, but not yet a society devoted to a still-living author. Nonetheless, and despite a certain jocular disbelief in the press, three hundred admirers turned up for the inaugural meeting. In America, where Browning had always been more popular, societies sprang up all over the place. As Ryals records in his biography, "his poems were printed on railway timetables in Chicago, where bookstores were unable to keep up with the demand for copies of his poems. In St. Louis a Sordello club was initiated. The Browning craze even manifested itself in clothing and interior decor, as brown dresses, brown curtains and brown bread became *de rigueur.*"[1]

The two volumes of *Dramatic Idyls* were well received and generally highly praised. The diction of the pieces is surprisingly lucid for Browning, and despite the fact that most of the poems in these two collections have the same twelve-syllabled rhyming couplets we find in the baffling *Fifine*, they move effectively along. Indeed, where before Browning dealt with his subjects in a grotesque style, here the style is straightforward enough but the subjects seem grotesque.

"Ned Bratts," for instance, retells an anecdote recorded in John Bunyan's seventeenth-century religious tract *The Life and Death of Mr Badman*. The scene is set vividly:

A broiling blasting June,—was never its like, men say.
Corn stood sheaf-ripe already, and trees looked yellow as that;
Ponds drained dust-dry, the cattle lay foaming around each flat.
Inside town, dogs went mad, and folk kept bibbing beer
While the parsons prayed for rain. (2–6)

While Bedford court is in session, Ned Bratts and his wife, Tabby, burst in and demand to be hanged. They declare that they had been criminals since youth and now wish to be brought to justice. Having been converted to Christianity, they consider confession of their sins followed swiftly by death to be the most effective way of getting straight to Heaven ("Heaven was above, and hell might rage in impotence / Below" [59–60]). Their physical ugliness ("horrified, hideous, frank fiend-faces" [56]) matches the litany of their crimes: drunkenness, theft, perjury, adultery. It becomes clear that the drought in Bedford stands for the moral and religious barrenness of the times; and when Ned and Tabby read Bunyan's *Pilgrim's Progress* they become aware of the potential for spiritual regeneration: "There's greenness yet at core, / Sap under slough!" (194–195). Water does eventually flow when Ned Bratts gets down on his knees:

wheezed a hoarse "Do hang us please!"
Why, then the waters rose, no eye but ran with tears,
Hearts heaved, heads thumped . . . (280–282)

And hanged they are.

But Browning, a lifelong opponent of capital punishment, would hardly be likely to celebrate that fact. "If Justice, on the spur," he comments in a passage added in proof, "Proved somewhat expeditious, would Quality demur?" (325–326). People of quality might not object, but it is difficult for the reader to avoid doing so. "Ned Bratts," then, functions as an ironic, even satirical story of anti-selflessness, of an apparent self-sacrifice that is in fact motivated purely by selfishness. Ned was converted by *The Pilgrim's Progress*, but he admits himself drunk when he read it—"I had to keep my whistle wet / While reading Tab this book" (106–107)— and his assumption that the only way out of sin is death is clearly untenable. The courtroom setting, the crucial interpretation of a text (Bunyan's), and the double death recall *The Ring and the Book*; "Ned Bratts" might stand as a *ratio inferior* to the larger undertaking, a brief and more comic excursus on the same themes of the slipperiness of interpretation and the near-impossibility of evenhanded judgment in this world.

Browning continued his newfound fascination with Greek myth in his shorter poems. "Pheidippides" and "Pan and Luna," from the first and second series of *Dramatic Idyls*, respectively, are both concerned with the god Pan, half man and half goat. In the former poem, Pan is a benevolent, indeed awe-inspiring figure—Browning underlines the characterization with a Greek-English pun on the god's name (*pan* in Greek means "all"): "majestical Pan! . . . All the great God was good in his eyes grave-kindly" (65–67). Pan in this poem is a heroic helper of mankind, in particular of Athens in the battle of Marathon. In "Pan and Luna," however, the god appears as a brutish figure who presses his amorous attentions on Luna, the goddess of the moon, whether she will or no: "So lay this Maid-Moon clasped around and caught / By rough red Pan, the god of all that tract" (65–66).

In "Pheidippides" Pan is a "God"; in "Pan and Luna" a "god." This downgrading is appropriate insofar as "Pan and Luna" includes a very physical and violent re-creation of a rape:

> Raked by his bristly boar-sward while he lapped
> —Never say kissed her! that were to pollute
> Love's language . . .
>   she recoiled—as who finds thorns
> Where she sought flowers—when feeling, she touched—horns!
>   (84–88)

The phallic imagery ("thorns," "horns") and the suggestive "raked" (raped? ploughed?) stress the sexual nature of what is going on. Equally important is the bestialization of Pan. He "laps" like an animal, despite the fact that his mouth is part of his human, indeed divine, half. His skin, likewise, is described as "boar-sward," his bestial part demoted from goat to pig. Browning seems to be suggesting the dualism, the double nature, which Pan represents; we might recall the phrase from Aeschylus quoted in *Fifine*: "God, man, or both together mixed." (2210)

Another mythical poem, "Ixion" (from *Jocoseria*, 1883), begins,

> High in the dome, suspended, of Hell, sad triumph, behold us!
> Here the revenge of a God . . .
> Whirling forever in torment, flesh once mortal, immortal
> Made—for a purpose of hate—able to die and revive
> Pays to the uttermost pang. (1–5)

Ixion, a mortal, was punished by Zeus by being strapped to a burning wheel forever. The apparent contradiction in Browning's first line here ("high" in "Hell") reflects an ambiguous myth. Ixion in some authorities is to be found deep in the underworld ("Thunderstruck, downthrust, Tartaros-doomed to the wheel," says Browning [112]). Yet elsewhere, in Pindar for instance, the wheelbound Ixion is sent spinning through the heavens as a warning message. This uncertainty (is Ixion above or below?) serves Browning's purpose. The course of the poem raises its hero up from lowest Erebos (85), "wrecked by his [Zeus's] weakness, I whirl. / Out of the wreck I rise" (120–121). The heroic mantle which Browning places on Ixion lifts him to the highest heaven, "whilst thou—Zeus, keep the godship and sink!" (124). More than one critic has commented on the fact that Browning's presentation of Ixion raises him from the out-and-out villain of the mythic original to the heights of a Shelleyan Prometheus, nobly enduring an unjust punishment.[2] Notably, although the mythic sources describe Ixion's crimes as ranging from attempted rape to hubris, Browning's Ixion is entirely blameless. Far from aspiring to the condition of the gods, he was content as a mortal. Instead, it was Zeus who aspired to humanity and attempted to use Ixion to achieve this aim: "I clothed, with the grace of our human, / Inhumanity—gods, natures I likened to ours" (73–74).

Browning's wordplay is slick: if mortal and immortal are interchangeable terms for man and god, respectively, Browning replaces "mortal" with its synonym "human" and then logically extrapolates "inhuman" from the antonym "immortal." "God" and "inhuman" are presented as sharing the same meaning. The whole poem, of course, illustrates the profound inhumanity, in the broadest sense, of Zeus's godhead. Ixion accuses him thus: "You aspire to be Man! Man made you who vainly would ape him: / You are the hollowness, he—filling you, falsifies void" (91–92).

Browning here is almost echoing Swinburne's sentiment on the same theme, in the latter's "Hymn to Man" (from *Songs before Sunrise*, 1871): "it is but for your sake that the God of your making is made. / Thou and I and he are not gods made men for a span, / But God, if a God there be, is the substance of men which is man" (42–44). But although Browning's and Swinburne's point may initially seem similar, in fact they diverge. Swinburne's aim is to stress atheistic self-reliance. For Browning, mortal men are superior to the Olympians precisely because they have access to a superior divine revelation. This argument is elaborated towards the end of Ixion:

When Man's strength proves weak, checked in the body or soul—
Whatsoever the medium, flesh or essence . . .
. . . clothing the entity Thou,
—Medium whence that entity strives for the Not-Thou beyond it . . .
   (100–104)

Although Zeus's strength is apparent in Ixion's punishment, by the end of the poem we realize that Zeus is acting out of weakness. Ixion, like Shelley's Prometheus, arrives at this conclusion and is filled with a sense of an "infinite Pure" existing above the tyrant Zeus. When he tries to "burst to the infinite Pure, / Nothing is reached but the ancient weakness still that arrests strength" (107–108). Asking himself "must I fall[?]," he is able to answer with a resounding pseudo-Christian "No": "for beyond, far, far is a Purity all-unobstructed! / Zeus was Zeus—not Man: wrecked by his weakness, I whirl. / Out of the wreck I rise—past Zeus to the Potency o'er him!" (119–121). Ixion's thoughts on "the Potency beyond Zeus" seem to recall Caliban's meditations on "the Quiet," "the something over Setebos / That made Him" ("Caliban upon Setebos," 129–130).

After a century of neglect, some of Browning's later works have been rescued by energetic critics championing misunderstood or unappreciated beauties. *Ferishtah's Fancies* (1884) is not such a work. Generally seen as among the weakest of Browning's productions, this collection of didactic tales put into the mouth of a fictional seventeenth-century Persian poet (the Ferishtah of the title) has failed to ignite a spark of enthusiasm in even the most faithful of Browning's readers. Yet even here there are things to admire. The vigorous prologue, for instance, sees Browning put his sheer love of good food into poetry:

> Pray Reader, have you eaten ortolans
> > Ever in Italy?
> Recall how cooks there cook them: for my plan's
> > To—Lyre with Spit ally.
> They pluck the birds,—some dozen luscious lumps,
> > Or more or fewer,—
> Then roast them, heads by heads and rumps by rumps,
> > Stuck on a skewer. (1–8)

Browning compares the way ortolans (a small game bird) are cooked—a number of them kebabbed on a skewer, bread and sage leaves interspersing the meat—with the way *Ferishtah's Fancies* is constructed, brief lyrics interspersing the fancies in a combination of "sense" and "song" (30). The queerness of the simile, spiced with outlandish rhymes ("Italy" / "Spit ally," "tattling" / "fatling," and so on), adds vigor to the straightforward poem. And it is in its lyrics that *Ferishtah's Fancies* manages some of its best moments.

> Fire is in the flint: true, once a spark escapes,
> Fire forgets the kinship, soars till fancy shapes
> Some befitting cradle where the babe had birth—
> Wholly heaven's the product, unallied to earth.
> Splendours recognized as perfect in the star!—
> In our flint their home was, housed as now they are.

The final rhyme of "star" / "are" recalls the end of Shelley's elegy for Keats, "Adonais" ("The soul of Adonais, like a star / Beacons from the abode where the Eternal are"). In a more abstract sense, Browning's little lyric makes a link similar to that of Shelley's huge elegy—between the apparently unpromising earthly arena and the heavenly splendor of the stars.

Indeed, one inescapable feature of Browning's later lyrics is the sheer potency of the presence of Shelley. The conventional view of Browning's poetic relationship with Shelley—that he was profoundly influenced in his youth but outgrew that influence and later repudiated Shelley altogether when he discovered what he considered dishonorable elements in the poet's treatment of his wife—is clearly inadequate. Browning may have passed through a period of disillusionment, yet his whole poetic corpus demonstrates how misleading the *ad hominem* argument can be. A poem such as "Reverie" from Browning's last publication, *Asolando* (1889) makes this plain.

"Reverie" may well be the last full poem Browning wrote; certainly it is one of the last, and as Pettigrew and Collins point out, "the temptation to see the poem as intended as a kind of last testament on subjects of central importance in Browning's philosophy is irresistible" (2.1130–1131).[3] Usually the poem has been read as a Christian work, rather too abstract to be successful. But in fact it seems clear that this is a poem in dialogue with Shelley's "Mont Blanc" (1816); and, as we might expect in a text that owes so much to the work of a noted atheist, it is difficult to describe "Reverie" as a Christian poem in any uncomplicated sense. The reverie itself begins as a meditation on the Shelleyan term "Power":

> I know there shall dawn a day
> —Is it here on homely earth?
> Is it yonder, worlds away,
> Where the strange and new have birth,
> That Power comes full in play? (1–5)

The syntax is somewhat mangled: the sentence that begins as a straightforward statement of fact ("I know") about the future ("shall dawn") becomes, incongruously, a question about the present ("That Power comes full in play?"). This should alert us to the fact that language, in true Browning style, is struggling as it tries to fit the infinite into the finite. The binary contrast between homely earth and the decidedly unhomely heavens (a contrast between body and soul) is elaborated with characteristic Browning distinctness:

> Is it here, with grass about,
> Under befriending trees,
> When shy buds venture out,
> And the air by mild degrees
> Puts winter's death past doubt?

> Is it up amid the whirl and roar
>> Of the elemental flame
> Which star-flecks heaven's dark floor,
>> That, new yet still the same,
> Full in play comes Power once more? (6–15)

What are we to make of this term, "Power"? Is it, like "the Potency" in "Ixion" or "the Quiet" in "Caliban upon Setebos," simply a name for the Christian God? If so, it's not in keeping with Shelley's use of the term in "Mont Blanc," a hymn to the sublime he wrote in the Vale of Chamouni after having gazed upon the splendid cataracts of the River Arve as it poured down from the glacial Alpine peak of Mont Blanc itself. To Shelley this river represents the way "the everlasting universe of things / Flows through the mind" (1–2). The Ravine of Arve ("dizzy Ravine!" the poet says, "when I gaze on thee / I seem as in a trance sublime and strange") ("Mont Blanc," 34–5) gives Shelley an inkling of a suprahuman governing force of the universe, a force which he calls "Power," or "Necessity." The River Arve provides his human mind with a means of apprehending the inapprehensible nature of this force. The scene he witnesses is "awful" in the literal sense, in that it is filled with awe:

> awful scene,
> Where Power in the likeness of the Arve comes down
> From the ice gulphs that gird his secret throne,
> Bursting through these dark mountains like the flame
> Of lightning through the tempest. (15–19)

Shelley's "Power" is very far from being a personalized Christian God; it is the impersonal force that orders the universe, unchangeable necessity, quite alien in nature to the perishable and changeable nature of humanity.

In "Reverie" Browning turns to this Shelleyan conception of ultimate necessity and seeks to relocate it within a more Christian framework. He wants to believe that there will be a day when this force will interact with "homely earth"; yet, as the syntax of the first stanza suggests, he cannot quite bring himself to assert as much. Like Shelley, he finds the concept too sublime, too mighty and distant, really to accommodate the "befriending trees" of springtime; it belongs more to the "star flecks" of "heaven's dark floor." Is Shelley's Power really God as Browning understands Him? Well, not really. "Power, once plain / Proved Power" (123–124), the poet notes; and he goes on to quote the opening of the Christian Bible ("In the beginning God / Made heaven and earth" [156–157]) not as a harmonious endorsement of Power's capabilities, but as a text which it remains the poet's job to "guess . . . the purport" of (153–154). With another reference to Mont Blanc, Browning acknowledges that it is impossible for the mind to withstand "the love-less Power" (184):

> No more than the passive clay
> Disputes the potter's act,
>   Could the whelmed mind disobey
> Knowledge the cataract. (187–190)

These are key lines. If the reference to the potter's wheel perhaps recalls Rabbi Ben Ezra's complacent comparison of God to a potter moulding mankind into a cup for His personal use, here the comparison has been invoked to rather different effect. Just as Shelley's mind in "Mont Blanc" is almost overwhelmed by the sheer enormity of the cataract of the Arve (or "Power in the likeness of the Arve"), so Browning asserts that try as he might to fit awful Power into the Christian paradigm of "God as Love," he can't resist the knowledge that Power is quite alien, quite other. The poem ends with a stanza that answers the questions posed in the opening. Is it on the homely earth that Power will become manifest? No, "not on the homely earth," but "worlds away, / Where the strange and new have birth" (217–219). Right to the end of his life, Browning was not content with simply inhabiting conventional Christian forms—and Shelley was still an important influence.

Asolando was published on the day that Browning died: December 12, 1889. Helped partly by the upsurge of emotion that the poet's death engendered, but also by the generally accessible and often charming lyrics of the volume itself, *Asolando* became a best-seller, going through four editions in a short time. A poem such as "Summum Bonum" ("the sum of all good things") seems straightforward and even touching, particularly when we remember that the poet was in his seventies when he wrote it.

> All the breath and the bloom of the year in the bag of one bee:
>   All the wonder and wealth of the mine in the heart of one gem:

In the core of one pearl all the shade and the shine of the sea:
    Breath and bloom, shade and shine,—wonder, wealth, and—
        how far above them
      Truth, that's brighter than gem,
      Trust, that's purer than pearl,
Brightest truth, purest truth in the universe—all were for me
In the kiss of one girl.

This sort of paean to the intensity of experience represented by a
lover's kiss has literary antecedents (we, might think of Leigh Hunt's
1838 rondeau beginning "Jenny kissed me" in particular). Yet the most
striking aspect of the poem is surely the anticlimactic effect of the last
line. The highest good, the sum of all good things, the apotheosis of the
world of growing things (the first line), of the beauties of the mineral
world (the second), and of the oceans (the third), as well as all the
abstract qualities that are then listed, all strung together in a highly
alliterative, single sentence . . . the effect is to create a tremendous sense
of build up. Even if we take "kiss" as a euphemism for more intimate
congress (underlined by the implicit reference to fertility in the first line,
to penetration in the second, and to the surrendering of chastity in the
third), it is difficult to agree with what the poet is suggesting.

    "Summum Bonum" doesn't really work. More in line with Brown-
ing's awareness of the dynamics of love relationships is the excellent
"Inapprehensiveness," in which two lovers fail to connect. In place of the
overstatement of a poem such as "Summum Bonum," this poem deals
masterfully with the fatal understatement that dooms the potential of
love between two lovers. It begins abruptly:

    We two stood simply friend-like side by side,
    Viewing a twilight country far and wide,
    Till she at length broke silence. "How it towers
    Yonder, the ruin o'er this vale of ours!" (1–4)

But the woman's observations on the scenery and her wondering
whether there is any passage in the works of John Ruskin that notice
"that certain weed-growths on the wall" (13) resemble something are
left hanging as the narrative perspective suddenly switches to inside the
man's head.

> Oh fancies that might be, oh facts that are!
> What of a wilding? By you stands, and may
> So stand unnoticed till the Judgement Day,
> One who, if once aware that your regard
> Claimed what his heart holds,—woke, as from its sward
> The flower, the dormant passion, so to speak—
> Then what a rush of life would startling wreak
> Revenge on your inapprehensive stare. (18–25)

The expert control of cadence in that last line, the way the lingering "inapprehensive" spools the line out, slows down the rather fevered meditations of the previous few lines, is the mark of a master. And despite the recognition in the poem that lovers who connect with one another can touch "Quietude—that's a universe in germ" (28), the poem as a whole articulates the non-connection, as represented by the wonderfully inconsequential closing lines:

> "No, the book
> Which noticed how the wall-growths wave" said she
> "Was not by Ruskin."
>   I said "Vernon Lee?" (30–32)

Vernon Lee was a minor nineteenth-century essayist and novelist, and the step down from the major Ruskin to this nonentity mirrors the slippage away from the possibility of "immense life" the couple is undergoing.

Chapter Ten

Parleyings with Certain People

A critic writing in 1886 reported that Browning had just "destroyed the whole of his letters to his father and family"; the reason was his "dreading his future biographer." At the same time, there was a rumor that he was working on his autobiography.[1] Writing his life story might have seemed an odd departure for Browning. In "House," Browning had forsworn the autobiographical:

> Outside should suffice for evidence,
>
> And whoso desires to penetrate
>
> Deeper, must dive by the spirit sense. (33–35)

When the autobiographical work finally emerged in 1887, critics and readers could be forgiven for not recognizing it as such. Indeed, it appears to be by far the most oblique and difficult of Browning's compositions since *Sordello*: a series of poems written in specific dialogue with obscure figures from the past and in which space is given to intricate meditation on a variety of abstruse themes. The title seems off-putting enough in its own right:

PARLEYINGS WITH CERTAIN PEOPLE
OF IMPORTANCE IN THEIR DAY

To wit: BERNARD DE MANDEVILLE,
DANIEL BARTOLI,
CHRISTOPHER SMART,
GEORGE BUBB DODINGTON,
FRANCIS FURINI
GERARD DE LAIRESSE
CHARLES AVISON

Introduced by
A DIALOGUE BETWEEN APOLLO AND THE FATES

Concluded by
ANOTHER BETWEEN JOHN FUST AND HIS FRIENDS

This list of names meant as little to readers in Browning's day as it does to us today; indeed, since both de Mandeville and Christopher Smart have enjoyed a small revival in their reputations recently, the people invoked were probably *more* obscure to the Victorians than they are to us. "People of Importance in Their Day" they may have been, but their contemporary lack of importance is one reason why Browning chose them. He invokes representative figures: philosopher, historian, poet, politician, priest, painter, and composer. But they are also people who influenced Browning at various stages during his life. By staging a poetic debate, or "parleying" with each in turn, Browning is able to explore his own artistic and intellectual origins and thereby sketch out a poetic version of his life. Of course, in the true Browning manner, this is autobiography in a very particular sense: it does not focus on the outward activities of a man, Robert Browning, but on the life and development of his mind, his soul.

The *Parleyings* are remarkably unforgiving in regard to the reader. The style is Browningese to the fullest extent, from the outrageous rhymes and hobbledy versification of the prologue and epilogue to the densely matted and inwoven texture of the rhymed pentameters that make up each parleying. The allusions are often so abstruse as to have baffled even expert editors of Browning, and the themes can seem strangely evanescent. Furthermore, it is an extremely ambitious piece of work in terms of form. As Ryals points out, it constitutes not only "an intellectual autobiography told in a familiar, conversational style," but it is also "of epic, encyclopedic scope—a kind of *Divina Commedia* rooted in *commedia dell'arte*."[2] It is useful, therefore, to have some sense of the overall shape or structure of the work.

Yet that is not easily attained because, on one level, the *Parleyings* resist being fitted into structural pigeonholes.[3] What is clear on analysis is that the *Parleyings* exhibit a progressive patterning, which is to say that in place of the circular, balanced pattern of a text such as *The Ring and the Book*, Browning strings his parleyings along a linear design, tending upwards. Each parleying builds, to a certain extent, upon the preceding, and the overall scheme traces a certain evolution. This linear scheme can be related to Browning's own life and, more important, to the development of his soul. If we look again at the list of figures invoked—philosopher, historian, poet, politician, priest, painter, composer—we might argue that Browning began as a philosopher (particularly in *Paracelsus*) and then wrote a historical work (*Sordello*) before becoming a poet in the more conventional sense of the term (*Men and Women*). His arguments with Elizabeth Barrett over politics (which resulted, eventually, in *Hohenstiel-Schwangau*) and his engagement with religion (which informed many of his poems) are then represented. Painting had always been an important love of Browning's, but became more so after his son, Pen, turned to painting as a career in 1874. Music comes last because, as the "Parleying with Avison" makes clear, Browning throughout his life considered it in some respects a superior form of art to poetry. The scheme leads us up from hard, crude thought (philosophy), through varieties of literary and artistic endeavor, through engagement with people's lives (politics and religion), to two nonverbal forms of art that supersede the literary.

Most important, perhaps, in a writer who had always been decidedly oppositional in his conception of reality, is the way the parleyings work dialectically, strophe and antistrophe, thesis and antithesis, moving toward an artistic and harmonious synthesis that can only be represented by the printed music with which "Avison" ends.

The prologue, "Apollo and the Fates," sets this scene partly by elaborating a host of binary oppositions. It looks back to an earlier work by Browning (*Balaustion's Adventure*) and a favorite myth of his: "Apollo and the Fates" dramatizes the premise of Euripides' play *Alkestis*. The three Fates have control over human lives, and Atropos is about to cut the thread of Admetus's life. Apollo descends to parley with the three goddesses and plead for a reprieve. The bargain eventually struck—Admetus may live if he can find somebody to die in his place—is the premise of the play and the focus of the prologue. In Browning's treatment, the fundamental binary division between male (Apollo) and female (the Fates) encompasses others: Apollo is high (the stage direction is "From above") and the Fates "low"; he is young (a "bright boy thing," a "youth" [81, 82]), they are old ("our eld" [81]); he is optimistic, they more cynical; he is arguing for life, they for death.

It is also important to isolate the basic shape of the prologue because its pattern is repeated in subsequent parleyings. Two events happen in the course of the poem to upset the balance created by the tension between Apollo and the Fates. The first is Apollo's offer of "Man's invention of—WINE!" (115) to the Fates. Never having previously encountered alcohol, they drink and are filled with the lightness and optimism that characterize Apollo. Drunk, they announce an end to their differences with the god ("Quashed be our quarrel" [201]). The second event is the *"explosion from the earth's centre"* (221–222), which reverses the effect of the first event. If the Fates came under the influence of Apollo's wine, they are immediately sobered by the chthonic eruption.

ATROPOS

Horror yawns under me, while from on high—humph!
    Lightnings astound, thunders resound,
Vault-roof reverberates, groans the ground! (*Silence*)

APOLLO

I acknowledge.

THE FATES

Hence, trickster! Straight sobered are we!
    The portent assures us 'twas our tongue spoke the truth,
Not thine. (223–228)

Apollo "submits" to the Fates, and the prologue ends with the victorious laughter of Atropos. This explosion is clearly of primary importance in the poem's construction as similar explosions from below recur throughout the *Parleyings*.

In the "Parleying with Christopher Smart," for instance, Browning uses such an image to describe the onset of Smart's "divine" madness:

    sane at starting: all at once the ground
Gave way beneath his step, a certain smoke
Curled up and caught him, or perhaps down broke
A fireball wrapping flesh and spirit both. (77–80)

In "Daniel Bartoli" the Duchess's marriage and "triumph" (122)—recalling the Fates's "no defeat but a triumph"—is overturned by "lo, a thunderclap!" (122). In "Gerard de Lairesse," Lairesse's "walk" through Greek mythology is heralded by "Thunders on thunders" and "a sharp white fire," when "circled with flame there yawned a sudden rift / I' the rock face" (181–189). The "Parleying with Charles Avison" also begins with the opening of a "cleft":

> this one cleft—
> —O what a life and beauty filled it up
> Startlingly, when methought the rude clay cup
> Ran over with poured bright wine! (11–14)

This "wine," which recalls Apollo's wine from the prologue, acts as a link between "Apollo" and "Avison."

The "cleft" calls to mind a much earlier chasm, one that occurs at the beginning of *Sordello* and through which fourteenth-century Verona is "hurled" into the domain of the poem:

> Lo, the past is hurled
> In twain: up-thrust, out-staggering on the world,
> Subsiding into shape, a darkness rears
> Its outline . . . (1.73–76)

At the other end of Browning's working life, a poem such as "Bad Dreams III" from *Asolando* records the similar image of a city broken by the growth, from beneath, of great trees:

> each oak
> Held on his horns some spoil he broke
> By surreptitiously beneath
> Upthrusting: pavements, as with teeth,
> Griped huge weed widening crack and split. (137–141)

The motifs of explosion and eruption, then, are not only common to the *Parleyings* but possess a long pedigree in Browning's work. For Browning, they represent perhaps the externalization of the inner upward thrust of the subconscious, the process by which poetic imagery imposes itself on the writer's conscious mind.

In the *Parleyings*, Greek myth is a recurring concern, with metaphors and examples taken from myth being used repeatedly to articulate the work's themes. The "Parleying with Bernard de Mandeville" is built around a debate between the narrator and the ghost of the recently demised Thomas Carlyle on the presence of evil in the world. Carlyle sees the existence of evil as a reason for pessimism; according to him, there is "no sign":

> No stirring of God's finger to denote
> He wills that right should have supremacy
> On earth, not wrong! How helpful could we quote
> But one poor instance where he interposed . . .
> Between oppression and its victim. (44–49)

In order to confute Carlyle's pessimism, Browning summons up the figure of Bernard de Mandeville; and the refutation takes the form of a retelling of the myth of Prometheus—a semidivine figure who, witnessing mankind's suffering, risked divine displeasure by bringing mankind the spark of fire. This, then, is the "one instance" of mankind being aided that Carlyle is asking for.

And yet it might be thought strange that Browning invokes the non-Greek de Mandeville rather than one of the great Greek tragedians, perhaps Euripides or Aeschylus (who are so important elsewhere in Browning) (206) to retell this Greek myth. It is stranger still when we remember that de Mandeville was the author of *The Fable of the Bees* (1724), a cynical and ironic treatise in which a comparison of mankind with the beehive leads to an assertion that selfishness is the foundation of a good commonwealth. De Mandeville was being satirical, and critics have assumed that Browning missed the point of the joke and took his work literally. But what the critics have missed is that Browning invokes de Mandeville as a necessary foil to Carlyle and that the work mentioned in the text (93) is not his *Fable of the Bees* but his poem *The Grumbling Hive* (1705). If Carlyle says that it is intolerable to live in a world of evil with no sign of goodness, de Mandeville in his poem argues that it is impossible to live in a world of goodness with no sign of evil:

> Then leave complaints. Fools only strive
> To make a Great an Honest Hive . . .
> Bare Virtue can't make Nations live
> In splendour; they that would revive
> A Golden Age, must be as free
> For Acorns, as for Honesty. (99–108)

The bulk of "Parleying with Bernard de Mandeville" is taken up with a reworking of the Prometheus myth. In this version, man is miserable because he cannot partake of the sun's "earth-felt thrill" (235) like the rest of creation. Browning casts his retelling as a lengthy (65 lines) monologue, possibly a speech written for a never-completed drama and then reassigned to the *Parleyings*. The complaint receives a succinct answer:

> Thus moaned
> Man till Prometheus helped him,—as we learn,—
> Offered an artifice whereby he drew
> Sun's rays into a focus,—plain and true,
> The very Sun in little; made fire burn. (301–305)

It has been argued that this lens or "artifice," which distills the solar "efflux" (297), represents the poetic craft, managing to mediate the infinite through the finite capacities of the poetic imagination.[4] Of course, Prometheus kindling fire with a glass lens is not to be found in any other version of the myth. It is Browning's own invention, a fact signaled by its anachronism (glassmaking was not at such an advanced stage of development in mythic or even historical Greece). It is important for those who think Browning was too dense to comprehend de Mandeville's (rather obvious) irony to realize that Browning's metaphor contains a fundamental contradiction. The "glass-conglobed" prism is used to create fire, yet fire is necessary to make glass in the first place. This chicken-and-egg double bind works to deconstruct the typical, unambiguous picture of a kindly Prometheus giving a helping hand to an overcomplaining humanity. The interrelation of good and evil, as Browning well knew, was much too complex to be solved by anything so banal. That Browning's focusing artifice is itself self-contradictory marks the presence of irony in the piece.

The next parleying is with Daniel Bartoli, an Italian Jesuit historian (1609–1685), whose histories (which Browning used more for the purpose of learning Italian than learning about the past) were so punctuated with descriptions of various miracles as to undermine their sense of historical veracity. The historical tale (based on fact) that Browning tells is of the way politics intervenes to destroy the otherwise happy relationship between Charles of Lorraine and Marianne Pajot. When Charles is made heir to the throne of France by Louis XIV's decree, the unofficial marriage between the two of them disintegrates under the strain of Charles' new political responsibilities. Refusing to accept certain royal instructions, Marianne breaks off the marriage; the Marquis de Lassay witnesses her diginified behavior and, despite the fact that he is only ten years old, forms an attachment for her. When he reaches twenty-three, the two marry despite the great disparity of age, and their few years together were very happy. The parleying functions as a celebration of "the divinest women that have walked / Our world" (1–2), presenting us with an idealized female principle in opposition to the idealized male Prometheus of "de Mandeville." The narrator's opinion that "man's best and woman's worst amount / So nearly to the same thing" (263–264) recalls the self-deprecating rhetoric Browning used during his courtship of Elizabeth Barrett, and it is difficult to avoid the conclusion that the story of a marriage between a virtuous older woman and an adoring younger man has autobiographical resonance for Browning. However, the lyric with which the parleying ends ("Who bade you come, brisk-marching bold she-shape") seems indisputably to invoke Lady Ashburton, and again the archetype of the ideal woman is subverted. Once more, Browning concludes his poem with a twist that throws an ironic light over the whole.

The next parleying—"with Christopher Smart"—returns us to a male figure. Nowadays Smart is mostly known as the author of a variety of poems written during his incarceration for madness (such as the "Jubilate Agno," the text of which was not discovered and published until 1939). For Browning and his contemporaries, Smart was a mediocre poet who had only written one good work; but that work, "A Song to David" (1763), was very highly regarded indeed. Writing in the *Athenaeum* (February 19, 1887), Dante Gabriel Rossetti declared that "this wonderful poem of Smart's is the only great *accomplished* poem of the last century . . . a masterpiece of rich imagery, exhaustive resources, and reverberant sound." To Browning it was all but incredible that a man whose collected works should contain so much dullness and second-rate work could also have produced so superb a poem. Browning sees "A Song to David" as the result of sudden and spontaneous inspiration, directly connected with the period of insanity Smart suffered in the middle of an otherwise dull career of versemaking. The metaphor Browning chooses to represent this is a walk through a large house. The house is plain, drably decorated, each room as boring as the one before. Suddenly the walker "flashingly emerge[s]" (37) into the chapel. This is the only bright and striking chamber in the house, however, and the walker then passes through another succession of grey rooms. This "dazzle," a poetic illumination, recalls the sun imagery from "de Mandeville"; once again Browning uses an Apollonian image of light to describe poetic achievement and completion (Apollo was god of poetry as well as of the sun). The epiphanic experience of reading "A Song to David" among the bulk of eighteenth-century poetry is suggested in the first few lines of the parleying, where uncertainty and questioning is briefly replaced by certainty and exclamation ("Let truth be said!") only to revert to questioning again:

> It seems as if . . . or did the actual chance
> Startle me and perplex? Let truth be said!
> How might this happen? Dreaming, blindfold led
> By visionary hand, did soul's advance
> Precede my body's[?] (1–5)

Smart "solely of such songmen pierced the screen / 'Twixt thing and word, lit language straight from soul . . . one blaze of truth" (113–117).

"Parleying with George Bubb Dodington" constitutes an exploration of the hypocrises inherent in the political process; in this and other respects it resembles the earlier *Prince Hohenstiel-Schwangau*. Dodington and the Prince use similar rhetoric. They characterize themselves as heroes, above the common man, if not quite gods—although, in the end, their phrasing smacks of mere elitism:

> High o'er Man's head we play,—and freelier breathe
> [Than] the multitude which gasps beneath . . .
> Ourselves at vantage to put forth a hand,
> Assist the prostrate public. (94–98)

As in *Schwangau* the political rhetoric undermines its own ends. Dodington suggests that he and those like him are the state's "disinterested slaves, nay—please the Fates— / Saviours and nothing less: Such lot has been!" (83–85). Hohenstiel-Schwangau similarly styled himself "saviour of society," but such a boast is out of place, as the accruing irony suggests. The messianic boast is made conditional ("please the Fates"), and, as the prologue has already asserted, the power and bias of these same goddesses are not subject to mortal demands or desires.

Francis Furini, in the next parleying, is placed before us as someone who, like Christopher Smart, expressed (Christian) divinity through his art; interestingly, the highest expression of his art is said to be the naked female form, the representation of which Browning consequently defends. In other words, the poem constitutes another hymn by Browning to the Superior Woman, this time through the perspective of the visual arts. The message is clearly stated: women deserve "reverence" because they are God's "supremest" creatures. The tone is familiar from Browning's early writings: art should

> endeavour to express
> Heaven's most consummate achievements, bless
> Earth by semblance of the seal God set
> On woman his supremest work. (131–134)

Furini was a seventeenth-century Italian who had been both a painter of nudes and a priest; but Browning is at least as concerned with his own son, Pen Browning, whose painted nudes had encountered criticism. In particular, his portrait of "Joan of Arc and the Kingfisher" (neither figure was clothed) had been attacked by the treasurer of the Royal Academy. Browning uses the parleying to address his son: "Painter! Fools attaint / Your fame . . . because its power inclines / To livelier colours" (549–551). The truth is that people attainted Pen's fame because he wasn't a terribly good painter, but Browning can perhaps be forgiven for thinking more highly of his son's abilities.

The lengthy description of a nude Joan of Arc at the end of the parleying serves another purpose apart from puffing Pen. Just as Furini is invoked at the beginning as a painter of nudes and as a priest ("a painter-priest" [3]), so Joan of Arc is presented both as a religious symbol and as a beautiful nude (the Duke D'Alençon is quoted: "though I saw while she undressed / How fair she was—especially her breast— / Never had I a wild thought" 591–593). But once again, the parleying has an ironic twist in its tail. First Browning introduces himself into the equation (quoting a "scribe" whose lines turn out to be verses written by Browning in 1886)—with this self-reflexiveness, the poem takes a slippery turn. The painting of St. Joan was not by Furini (actually it was by Penini), but nonetheless Browning credits it to the painter-priest. And no sooner has he done so than he asserts the painter-priest incapable of doing what he has been described as doing (that is, of capturing the divinity of the naked female form)—"that task's beyond you":

Paint this! Only turn
Her face away—that face is about to burn
Into an angel's when the time is ripe!
That task's beyond you. Finished, Francis?
Wipe Pencil, scrape palette,
and retire content! (611–615)

This final invocation to erasure has the effect of undoing, of deconstruct-
ing all that has been said: painting had been invoked as capturing the
divine essence, but now we discover that it cannot. As the text unravels
itself, collapses under a series of those gaps in understanding modern
critical thinking calls "aporias," we have to retire along with the painter.

"Gerard de Lairesse," the subject of the next parleying, was also a
painter; a Dutch artist (1641–1711) who went blind in late life and
wrote a treatise called *The Art of Painting in All Its Branches*. Browning
had read this work when a boy and been particularly struck by an imaginary walk de Lairesse took through all the appropriate situations and
scenarios for artistic treatment. De Lairesse championed the eternal relevance of the classics; most critics have seen this parleying as Browning's
repudiation of Lairesse's classicism. But it is nothing of the sort. The
lines that lead to this false impression come near the end, where Browning announces, "The dead Greek lore lies buried in the urn / Where who
seeks fire finds ashes" (392–393). But this is not a blanket denunciation
of Greek myth. Browning is talking about one very specific aspect of
Greek belief, namely the lack of any positive afterlife in Greek religion.
According to Greek theology, at death a person becomes what Browning, quoting Homer, describes as "a shade, a wretched nothing,—sad,
thin, drear" (395). Browning as a Christian cannot help but compare the
Greek conception with what he considers the "truth" of his own faith;
the "Greek lore" on "the dead" is cosmically pessimistic:

The dead Greek lore lies buried in the urn
Where who seeks fire finds ashes. Ghost forsooth!
What was the best Greece babbled of as truth?
"A shade, a wretched nothing,—sad, thin, drear,
Cold, dark, it holds on to the lost loves here["]
. . . Sad school
Was Hades! (392–404)

The parleying may reject Greek pessimism about death, but it positively revels in Greek literary art, exploring one by one all the major genres of classical literature. Browning, following de Lairesse's model, embarks on a walk through a variety of classical landscapes and also, it quickly transpires, through the gamut of classical modes. Indeed, the parleying reproduces in miniature the linear, progressive structure of the parleyings as a whole.

The narrational walk passes through times of the day (dawn, morning, noon, sunset) and various landscapes, each of which is associated with a distinct classical mode. It begins at dawn with Prometheus and drama: "I saw a form erect / Front and defy the outrage . . . Morn is breaking there— / The granite ridge pricks through the mist" (189–207). Then the narrator moves on to describe Artemis, the huntress-goddess of the moon—"supreme one, rightly called / Moonmaid in heaven above and, here below, / Earth's huntress queen" (229–231)—in an epic style redolent with allusions to and quotations from Homer. The first two figures invoked also recapitulate the contrast of the first and second parleyings (heroic Prometheus and Superior Woman). The third scene evokes the pastoral, derived from the Greek bucolic poet Moschus, and concerns the love between Pan and Echo (262–307). Browning then introduces a historical perspective by focusing on Alexander the Great and King Darius (332–333). Having adumbrated the dramatic, the epic, the idyllic and the historical, Browning is done with the major genres of Greek literature, but his walk is not over yet.

The heroic figures from the past cause him to reflect that "heroes tread the world's dark way no longer" (358), and the poem embarks upon

> my last adventure! 'Tis a ghost.
> So drops away the beauty! There he stands
> Voiceless, scarce strives with deprecating hands. (360–362)

The hands are deprecating the pitiful state of the ghost in the ancient and pagan scheme of afterlife: "Be death with me, as with Achilles erst / Of Man's calamities the last and worst" (409–410). The reference to Achilles is an allusion to the *Odyssey*, Book 11, where the shade of Achilles pitifully complains that he would rather return to earth as the meanest slave than reign as king of all the lands of the dead. But in "de Lairesse" Browning counters Greek pessimism with Christian positive thinking:

> Be proved potency that still
>
> Makes perfect, be assured, come what come will
>
> What once lives never dies . . .
>
> . . . What's death then? (411–416)

"De Lairesse" does not dismiss Greek myths (which Browning calls "true wonders" [68]); but it does acknowledge their inherent pessimism.

In the final parleying, "With Charles Avison," Browning, like Moses, looks into a promised land. Here, despite his lifetime of poetry, he announces that the highest form of art is music; and he does so without equivocation: "I state it thus: / There is no truer truth obtainable / By Man than comes of music" (137–139). The parleying ends resolutely with a musical score, as if to demonstrate this observation. Avison was an organ composer (1710–1770); his "Grand March" is reproduced by Browning. It is a bang-bang-bang sort of tune, in the key of C (we might almost say "the C-major of life"), to be played— according to the score—"lustily." Once again, the end of the parleying rather undermines the effect of the bulk of the text. In the body of the parleying Browning asserts that art, in general, seeks to "arrest Soul's evanescent moods, and keep / Unalterably still the forms that leap" (211–212). Achieving this most succesfully is music, consequently the highest form of art; and Avison's march, which apparently has Browning "entranced" (92), is a prime example. But Avison's plonky, clumsy music just isn't any good. It is difficult to escape the conclusion that the musically literate Browning was aware of this fact and cites the music as another end-of-parleying deflating or ironizing gesture.

There is an insistence throughout the *Parleyings* on reconciliation and synthesis. The very name, "parleyings," carries the implication of a parley, "a discussion of terms with an enemy with a view to ending conflict" (*Oxford English Dictionary*). Though all the figures mentioned are male, the title specifies humanity in general rather than maleness—*People of Importance*, not *Men of Importance*. As the poem progresses and its chief centers of interest become evident, the drawing together of opposites is clearly emphasized.

As mentioned above, the prologue is shot through with seemingly irreconcilable oppositions. The male/female distinction in "Apollo and the Fates" (and, arguably, in most of Browning's corpus) encompasses also the oppositional pairings of high/low, good ("weal")/"bad" ("woe"), and youth/age. But Apollo's offer of wine to the three goddesses initiates a drawing together of these contradictions. Lachesis, who has been weaving the cloth of fate, reconsiders the distinction between "pied" and "plain" in her weaving: "In a trice from the pied to the plain in my woof! / What parts each from either? A hair's breadth, no inch" (136–137). Black and white draw together: Lachesis declares that "Though on black next foot falls," it does not matter: "firm I fix it, nor flinch, / —Such my trust white succeeds!" (139–140). The point is not that opposites (good and evil, say, or black and white) become mixed together, but that it becomes possible to see each in proper relation to the other.

This is the sort of synthesis (effected by wine, "Earth's yield") which the *Parleyings* espouse. Apollo states the case in terms of a question: "Earth's yield, by Man's skill, can effect / Such a cure of sick sense that ye spy the relation / Of evil to good?" (141–143). At the beginning of "de Mandeville," the first parleying, we seem to get an answer to this question of good and evil. The narrative voice of that poem praises the "subtler skill" that, using logic, could

> sound deep, deeper, till
> It touched a quietude and reached a shrine
> And recognized harmoniously combine
> Evil with good, and hailed truth's triumph. (6–9)

This little passage acts almost as a commentary on the action of the prologue that immediately preceded it. The omnipotent "quietude" (which sounds, once again, like Caliban's "Quiet") is to be found a great way down, "deep, deeper." It was from such a subterranean shrine—the earth's center, to be exact—that the resonating "explosion" emanated, an explosion which took place immediately after the drunken Fates had hailed human life "a triumph." The paralleling is too close to be accidental. Browning is taking pains to suggest an all-powerful force, located not in the high heavens of patriarchal theism, but deep underground. This powerful "quietude" intervenes to restore the balance between the female Fates and the male god.

The same word, "quietude," is used oxymoronically to describe the speech of the Duchess in the "Parleying with Daniel Bartoli":

> At the table's head
> Where, 'mid the hushed guests, still the duke sat glued
> In blank bewilderment, his spouse pursued
> Her speech to end—syllabled quietude. (180–183)

The ode at the end of "Bartoli," hymning as it does a powerful, superior femme fatale, underlines female dominance. Christopher Smart's advice at the end of his parleying is simple enough—"Cease from anger at the fates . . . Live and learn" (263–264). Although uncapitalized, this reference to the Fates suggests the potency of those goddesses.

The epilogue to the *Parleyings*, "Fust and his Friends," celebrates John Fust, one of the first men to utilize a printing press (and the first man to print a book with a complete date. The book was a Psalter, printed on August 14, 1457, the date Browning chooses for his epilogue). Indeed, Browning all but gives Fust the credit for the invention of the printing press and then weaves a jolly tale in which Fust is confused with Faust (who sold his soul to the devil). Friends, alarmed at Fust's apparently magical ability to copy texts perfectly at tremendous speed, come by to try and save him from Satan. They muster their meager Latin for an exorcism, but Fust with two words of Greek sums up his achievement: "Move world! I have gained my '*pou sto*'! / I am saved" (190–191). The Greek is quoted from Archimedes and means "somewhere to stand." Archimedes experimented with levers and came to the conclusion that, given a place to stand and a sufficiently long lever, he could lift any weight, even that of the world. This conclusion, the reaching of a haven of objective certainty, provides an echo of the beginning of the *Parleyings*. Typical of this collection, however, there is a contextual irony in Fust's assertion. "A place to stand" recalls the first noun of the entire poem, "footfall," and the prologue makes plain that one cannot be certain what lies underneath such a *pou sto*.

Chapter Eleven
Browning's Reputation

For some years after his death, Browning's reputation was in the hands of the Browningites. The Browning Society published proceedings, and although the last public meetings were in 1892, private meetings and various other societies (particularly on the other side of the Atlantic) carried on the work. This work tended to portray Browning as a purveyor of great religious, if not exactly philosophical, truths. Sir Henry Jones's 1891 study has the sort of title that one simply doesn't find today: *Browning as a Philosophical and Religious Teacher*. Jones considers Browning's religion to be rather more coherent and rigorous than his philosophy, but nonetheless detects "profound error" in both. The underlying critical rationale is that Browning had certain nuggets of truth that he wished to convey directly to his audience, like happy pills, and which could therefore be assessed as right or wrong. A like-minded work is John Robertson's *Browning and Tennyson as Religious Teachers* (1903). This emphasis on Browning as a didactic artist, misrepresentative though it undoubtedly is, nevertheless adversely affected Browning's reputation, particularly as Victorianism became a musty, antiquated quantity and Modernism turned its back on the past.

Interestingly, the midwife of Modernism, Ezra Pound, was profoundly influenced by Browning and by *Sordello* in particular. We may take with a pinch of salt his claim that he read straight through Browning's epic the first time without pause, but the significance of the dramatic monologue as form for a great variety of Modernist poetic undertakings—T. S. Eliot's *The Waste Land*, Pound's *The Cantos*, David Jones's *In Parenthesis*, and so on—is incalculable. Yet Browning's critical reputation slid further and further down, as if the poet were being made to stand in the corner of the classroom with a placard around his neck saying "God's in his heaven— / All's right with the world!" George Santayana's chapter on Browning in his *Interpretations of Poetry and Religion* (1900) was called "The Poetry of Barbarism" and did much to damage Browning's reputation. For Santayana, the grotesque is one thing, barbarism quite another. "If energy and actuality are all that we care for," he says sternly, "chaos is as good as order, and barbarism as good as dis-

cipline." But "if the powers of the human mind are at any time adequate
to the task of digesting experience, clearness and order inevitably super-
vene . . . it is only at such periods that the human animal vindicates his
title of rational." And Browning?

> We are in the presence of a barbaric genius, of truncated imagination, of
> a thought and an art inchoate and ill-digested, of a volcanic eruption that
> tosses itself quite blindly and ineffectually into the sky.[1]

G. K. Chesterton (1903) attempted a defence of Browning as an artist,
but the tide was flowing in the opposite direction. Some scholarly articles excepted, it was not until after World War II that Browning's reputation began its slow re-ascent.

Important groundwork was done by William DeVane, whose encyclopedic *A Browning Handbook* (1935; the second edition came out in
1955) remains indispensable to Browning scholars. Indeed, it sometimes
seems as if DeVane single-handedly carried the torch for Browning criticism during the interwar period, not only with a variety of influential
articles (most notably "The Virgin and the Dragon" [*Yale Review* 37
(1947–1948), 33–46], which details Browning's fascination with the
myth of Perseus and Andromeda), but with a lengthy still-useful study
of the *Parelyings, Browning's Parleying: The Autobiography of a Mind*
(1927).

During the fifties, scholars began studying Browning in terms of his
formal and stylistic innovations. Yet William Raymond, in his essay
"The Infinite Moment" (from *The Infinite Moment and Other Essays in
Robert Browning*, 1950), can still observe that "though it is now sixty-five
years since the death of Robert Browning, the time is yet unripe for a
definitive estimate of his place amongst English men of letters." Even in
the fifties, Raymond complained, "the baiting of Victorianism continues
to be a favourite sport" among critics. Raymond points out that "a study
of the didactic interests of Browning leads to the periphery rather than
the centre," and instead advanced a reading of Browning's energetic
attempts to "put the infinite within the finite":

> It is precisely the dash or verve of his poetry which constitutes its peren-
> nial originality or attractiveness. . . . We are reminded of the violent rush
> of a mountain torrent frothing and seething amongst rocks and fretting
> its channel, but compensating for its lack of smooth rhythmical flow by
> the spin and dance, the spray and the sparkle of its waters. (3–18)

As this quotation illustrates, there is in this study, as in much early Browning scholarship, a tendency toward impressionistic criticism; but Raymond also has a series of fundamental insights into Browning's technique. For instance, his realization that "the relation between the form and the content of the poetry of Browning is often a tension rather than a harmony."

Another influential study from this time period is Robert Langbaum's *The Poetry of Experience: The Dramatic Monologue in Modern Literary Tradition* (1957). Langbaum examines the dramatic monologue as a formal poetic innovation, producing not a taxonomy but a critical study. His detailed reading of "My Last Duchess" is particularly good:

> The utter outrageousness of the duke's behaviour makes condemnation the least interesting response, certainly not the response that can account for the poem's success. What interests us more than the Duke's wickedness is his immense attractiveness ... We suspend moral judgement because we prefer to participate in the duke's power and freedom, in his hard core of character fiercely loyal to itself. Moral judgement is in fact important as the thing to be suspended. ["My Last Duchess"] carries to the limit an effect peculiarly the genius of the dramatic monologue—I mean the effect created by the tension between sympathy and judgement. (75–108)

Langbaum manages to sidestep the sort of purely judgmental arguments that Browning's monologues still tended to encourage. An example is the debate as to whether the Duke in "My Last Duchess" intends to reveal himself as a murderer or does so inadvertently. B. R. Jerman's "Browning's Witless Duke" (*PMLA* 72 [1957], 488–493) argues the latter point and is answered by Laurence Perrine's "Browning's Shrewd Duke" (*PMLA* 74 [1959], 157–159). But during the sixties the emphasis shifted away from such "character studies," and Browning was studied from more stylistic, formal, and theoretical perspectives.

J. Hillis Miller was to become a prime exponent of American deconstruction, but his long chapter on Browning in his *The Disappearance of God* (1963) predates this stage of his career. Instead, we are given a detailed reading of Browning's poetic technique and its broader implications. Miller's overall argument in this book (which considers five nineteenth-century writers) is that the Victorian age saw God withdrawing from the world not so much in terms of mass conversions to atheism (Browning was, after all, a Christian to the end), but in the sense of Nietzsche's 1882 claim "God is Dead"—which is to say, the loss of epistemological and metaphysical certitude, the encroachment of relativism. Miller's sense of how Browning uses language is particularly good:

> The first principle of Browning's poetry is his attempt to make the words of the poem participate in the reality they describe, for he seeks to capture the "stuff / O' the very stuff, life of life, and self of self." He wants words to be thick and substantial, and to carry the solid stuff of reality. He wants, as he said in a striking phrase, "word pregnant with thing." To read a poem by Browning should be a powerful sensuous experience, a tasting and feeling, not a thinking . . . He thinks of matter, in whatever form, as something dense, heavy, rough, and strong flavored . . . Grotesque metaphors, ugly words with heavy consonants, stuttering alliteration, strong active verbs, breathless rhythms, onomatopoeia, images of rank smells, rough textures, and of things fleshy, viscous, sticky, nubbly, slimy, shaggy, sharp, crawling, thorny, or prickly—all these work together in Browning's verse to create an effect of unparalleled thickness, harshness, and roughness. (Miller, *Disappearance of God*, 120)

Toward the end of the sixties, some of Browning's larger, which is to say longer, achievements came in for serious treatment. Richard Altick and James Loucks, for instance, produced an excellent and remarkably comprehensive study of *The Ring and the Book* (*Browning's Roman Murder Story*, 1968), in which they assert that "only by giving equally serious attention to all twelve of the books" can one "grasp Browning's full design." Their reading of the work as a baroque masterpiece emphasizes the tremendous structural and architectonic qualities of the poem. (1)

W. David Shaw's *The Dialectical Temper* (1968) analyzed what it called "The Rhetorical Art Of Robert Browning," which is to say, "the rhetorical art of engaging an audience and controlling its responses."[2] Shaw looks at the overall shape of Browning's career up to and including *The Ring and the Book* via close readings of a wide range of poems. My study is in keeping with his approach: he profiles a dialectic (hence the title) wherein the "Subjective Poet's problem" (evident in *Pauline* and *Paracelsus*) is in dialogue with the "Search for Objective form." Shaw's work has been particularly influential in its implicit contention that a critic needs to have a sense of the shape of Browning's career in order to understand the full implications of his dramatic monologues.

Harold Bloom, following his own influential theory of poetic influence (founded upon the notion that a great poet necessarily misreads his or her forebears), saw in Browning's relationship to Shelley a classic example.[3] Bloom's reading of Browning, in particular his almost obsessive fascination with "Childe Roland to the Dark Tower Came," has produced a great deal of powerful and memorable criticism. Bloom remains one of the most highly regarded of contemporary critics; though his essays on Browning make up but a small proportion of his overall output, they are well worth reading.

1974 saw the publication of the best of Browning biographies. *The Book, the Ring and the Poet* was begun by William Irvine and completed after his death by Park Honan. This remains the standard biography despite a variety of more recent biographical studies; it is admirably comprehensive and contains a great deal of critical readings.

The later 1970s and the 1980s saw the entry into Browning studies of deconstructionist critics. It probably does not overstate the case to argue that deconstruction, and related academic rhetorics, has effected something of a paradigm shift in Browning studies. Previous studies tended toward discussion of ethics or character or formalist analysis of Browning's contribution to the dramatic monologue. Studies from and since the eighties have embarked upon seeing Browning, preeminently among Victorian poets, as articulating the hermeneutic and epistemological aporias (the gaps or disconnections of the process of deriving knowledge) inherent in the textualizing of experience or (indeed) in any perception. The very qualities of Browning's verse that nineteenth-century critics found so problematic—the difficult style, the intractable treatment of form—become modern virtues, continually making readers aware of the insufficiency of any text to wholly apprehend reality.

Two books by the same author illustrate this deconstructionist shift fairly well. E. Warwick Slinn's *Browning and the Fictions of Identity* (1982) is a book chiefly in dialogue with Robert Langbaum. The book examines the way Browning's characters talk themselves into existence—the textuality of personality—and sees the poems as dramatic strategies, attempts to elaborate the necessary fictionalizing of identity. While Slinn's approach parallels contemporary deconstructionist criticism, his bibliography refers back to critics such as Langbaum and Northrop Frye. By the time of his next book, *The Discourse of Self in Victorian Poetry* (1991), however, Slinn had adopted the vocabulary of the new theorists to look at the ways major Victorian poetry (Browning in particular) mediates the "shift" "from Hegel to Derrida":

> This book reads Victorian poetry within the context of a radical shift over the last 150 years in the key European model for human definition and experience: from the metaphor of self to the metaphor of text. The

movement in thought from Hegel to Derrida produces a shift in the
dominating metaphor for human experience from consciousness as self
(there is nothing outside self) to consciousness as writing (there is nothing outside text). When placed within this changing process of media-
tion, Victorian poetry develops the problematics of selfhood, pursuing a
post-Romantic displacement of the self as an originary guarantor of
meaning and truth. (1)

In this scheme, Victorian literature assumes a particularly important
role as the mediator between Romanticist and Modernist/Postmodernist
aesthetics; and of all the Victorians Browning is the best suited to
deconstructionist reassessments. His dramatic monologues are clearly
aware of the problematics of selfhood; and his dense stylistic fabric
seems to depend on a conception of identity as textual.

Consequently, a great deal of more recent work on Browning has
benefited from the ructions theory has wrought on the traditional critical disciplines. This present study, as should be plain, has taken a fair
amount of theoretical material on board, but considers it anachronistic
to see Browning as wholly the deconstructionist *avant la lettre*. He may
have been an eloquent demonstrator of the contingent nature of human
endeavor, but he also believed in a divine and entirely objective reality in
God, which we all (he would have said) will have access to after our
deaths.

Herbert Tucker's very highly regarded *Browning's Beginnings: The Art
of Disclosure* (1980) is not deconstructionist in a doctrinaire sense, but it
does acknowledge the usefulness of Derrida (for instance) in understanding exactly where Browning's effectiveness lies. Tucker's chief insight
concerns the way Browning's poetry resists closure. Meaning is not contained, closed off, or restricted; rather, meaning is opened out, *dis*closed
rather than *en*closed:

> By putting the infinite within the finite through the use of a style that
> acknowledges its own insufficiency, Browning styles himself a romantic
> poet in full pursuit of the sublime . . . Sublimity for Browning entails not
> the traditional sending up, but a sending out or across . . . his poetry is
> most often horizontal in thrust, and it intensifies at moments when the
> negotiation of a frontier marks a new beginning. Meaning breaks into the
> lives of his characters as it breaks out of the phenomena in his world. (15)

Tucker's approach is not simply concerned with the effectiveness of
Browning's style (as in this quotation); it illuminates the whole of

Browning's poetics, from his insistence that there is a life after death (death being a moment of disclosure, of opening out) to his consistent representation of villainy as that which tries to contain and stifle.

Tucker's study is excellent, although it perhaps shows too little awareness of the cultural and historical contexts in which Browning worked. This is perhaps the largest gap in contemporary Browning studies. There have been many studies that interrogate the interrelationship between Browning's biography and his poetic production (Clyde Ryals's recent *The Life of Robert Browning* [1993] is a good example), but there has been very little work that puts Browning fully in the cultural context of the Victorian period. Loy D. Martin's Marxist study *Browning's Dramatic Monologues and the Post-Romantic Subject* (1985) attempts to place Browning's dramatic monologues in a political context; and Isobel Armstrong's detailed and powerfully argued *Victorian Poetry: Poetry, Poetics and Politics* (1993) does locate Browning among his poetic fellows. But a full-blown historicist study of Browning remains to be undertaken.[4]

Notes and References

Chapter 1

1. Quoted in Sutherland Orr, *Life and Letters of Robert Browning*, new ed. (London, 1908), 378–379.
2. Alfred Domett, quoted in Frederick Kenyon, ed., *Robert Browning and Alfred Domett* (London, 1906), 141.
3. See DeVane, *A Browning Handbook*, 244.
4. The "Essay" is reprinted in Pettigrew and Collins, *Poems*, 1:1001–13.
5. Browning's note is quoted in many places—see Woolford and Karlin, eds., *The Poems of Browning*, 1.15–16.
6. *Pauline* is quoted from the first published edition of 1833 and not the subsequent revised edition. See Woolford and Karlin, eds., *The Poems of Browning*, 1.14–26.
7. Quoted in Woolford and Karlin, eds., *The Poems of Browning*, 1.16–17.
8. See, for instance, Ryals, *The Life of Robert Browning*, 22, 254 n.2.

Chapter 2

1. The simile is not mine—see Ian Jack, *Browning's Major Poetry* (Oxford: Clarendon, 1973), 22.
2. See Woolford, *Browning the Revisionary*.
3. Quoted from a letter to Moncair, 1834, in Kelley and Hudson, eds., *The Browning Correspondence*, 3.125–130. Hereafter cited in the text as *Correspondence*.
4. Quoted in Woolford and Karlin, eds., *The Poems of Browning*, 1.240.
5. Quoted from a letter to Frederick Furnivall, October 11, 1881, in William S. Peterson, ed., *Browning's Trumpeter*, 34.
6. Irvine and Honan, *The Book, the Ring and the Poet*, 52.
7. For contemporary reactions, see also Litzinger and Smalley, eds., *Browning: The Critical Heritage* (London: Routledge and Kegan Paul, 1970) and Irvine and Honan, *The Book, the Ring and the Poet*, 86–87.
8. Quoted in Litzinger and Smalley, eds., *Browning: The Critical Heritage*, 84.
9. These and subsequent quotations from the Ruskin-Browning letters are taken from David DeLaura, "Ruskin and the Brownings: Twenty-Five Unpublished Letters," *Bulletin of the John Rylands Library* 54 (1972), 324–327.

10. See in particular Raymond, *The Infinite Moment and Other Essays in Robert Browning*, and Tucker, *Browning's Beginnings*.

Chapter 3

1. See Kintner, ed., *The Letters of Robert Browning and Elizabeth Barrett, 1845–46*, 241. Hereafter cited in the text as "Kintner." The Biblical reference to which Browning alludes is *Exodus* xxviii:33–35.

2. For more information about the dramatic monologue see Alan Sinfield, *The Dramatic Monologue* (1977); A. D. Culler, "Monodrama and the Dramatic Monologue," *PMLA* 90 (1975), 366–385.

3. Honan, *Browning's Characters: A Study in Poetic Technique* (New Haven, 1961), 122.

4. For a detailed study of the place of the dramatic monologue in the nineteenth-century development of "mental sciences," see Ekbert Faas, *Retreat into the Mind: Victorian Poetry and the Rise of Psychiatry* (Princeton, N.J.: Princeton University Press, 1988).

5. See Litzinger and Smalley, eds., *Browning: The Critical Heritage*, 185.

6. Tucker, *Browning's Beginnings*, 151.

7. Langbaum, *The Poetry of Experience*, 80.

8. B. Jerman, "Browning's Witless Duke," *PMLA* 72 (1957), 488–493; L. Perrine, "Browning's Shrewd Duke," *PMLA* 74 (1959), 157–159. For a more balanced view see Woolford, *Browning the Revisionary*, 71–72.

9. The quotation is in H. Corson, *An Introduction to the Study of Robert Browning*, 3rd ed. (Boston, 1903), viii.

Chapter 4

1. Quoted in Irvine and Honan, *The Book, the Ring and the Poet*, 158.

Chapter 5

1. Quoted from letters to Joseph Milsand (February 24, 1853) and Edward Chapman (March 5, 1853), in Irvine and Honan, *The Book, the Ring and the Poet*, 335.

2. Quoted from a letter to Chapman, December 17, 1855, in DeVane and Knickerbocker, eds., *New Letters of Robert Browning*, 85.

3. J. Hillis Miller, *The Disappearance of God*, 119–120.

4. See, for instance, Robert Pearsall, *Robert Browning* (Twayne, 1974), 80: "Musical Composition for Galuppi . . . had become, as Browning urges, a lifeless arithmetical exhibition, and its only valid message is that living things must die."

Chapter 6

1. See Ryals, *The Life of Robert Browning*, 134.

2. See *Browning's Hatreds*, 47–67.

Chapter 7

1.   See Litzinger and Smalley, eds., *Browning: the Critical Heritage*, 317.
2.   See Shaw, "Browning's Murder Mystery: *The Ring and the Book* and Modern Theory," 79; and Slinn, *The Discourse of Self in Victorian Poetry* (London: Macmillan, 1991), 119, 184.
3.   *Critical and Miscellaneous Essays*, ii.87.

Chapter 8

1.   Pearsall, *Robert Browning*, 130; Ryals, *The Life of Robert Browning*, 183; Irvine and Honan, *The Book, the Ring and the Poet*, 461.
2.   The exception is Loy Martin's *Browning's Dramatic Monologue and the Post-Romantic Subject.*
3.   *Theses on Feuerbach*, 157.
4.   *The Focusing Artifice*, 173.
5.   "Browning and the Poetry of Sexual Love," in Armstrong, ed., *Writers and Their Background: Robert Browning* (London, 1974), 295.
6.   There is virtually no worthwhile criticism of this tremendous poem. Karlin's *Browning's Hatreds* (147–168) provides one notable exception.
7.   James, in Litzinger and Smalley, eds., *Browning: The Critical Heritage*, 415; Ryals, *The Life of Robert Browning*, 200–201.

Chapter 9

1.   Ryals, *The Life of Robert Browning*, 218.
2.   See for instance Douglas Bush, *Mythology and the Romantic Tradition* (New York, 1969), 378–379: "Like Shelley's Prometheus, though not sinless, Ixion . . . proves himself greater than the tyrant . . . He has become, in short, a Christian."
3.   Pettigrew and Collins, eds., *Robert Browning: The Poems*, 2.1130–1131. The manuscript date is unclear, although it might be "14th October 1889," the day before Browning posted it to London for publication.

Chapter 10

1.   This information appeared anonymously in *The Critic*, January 2, 1886; it is quoted in Pearsall, *Robert Browning*, 164.
2.   Ryals, *The Life of Robert Browning*, 224.
3.   The issue of structure has been addressed by DeVane, *Browning's Parleyings: The Autobiography of a Mind* (New Haven, 1927) and by Mark Siegchrist, "Type Needs Antitype: The Structure of Browning's *Parleyings*," *Victorian Newsletter*, 50 (1976), 1–10.
4.   This is the central argument of Roma King's *The Focusing Artifice*.

Chapter 11

1. Quoted in Litzinger and Knickerbocker, eds., *The Browning Critics*, 57.
2. Shaw, *Dialectical Temper*, 1.
3. See his *Anxiety of Influence, a Theory of Poetry* (Oxford: Oxford University Press, 1973). For essays on Browning, see his *The Ringers in the Tower: Studies in the Romantic Tradition* (Chicago: University of Chicago Press, 1971).
4. An honorable exception is to be found in David DeLaura's "The Context of Browning's Painter Poems: Aesthetics, Polemics, Historics."

Selected Bibiliography

PRIMARY SOURCES

Individual Works

Pauline. A Fragment of a Confession (London: Saunders & Otley, 1833)
Paracelsus (London: Effingham Wilson, 1835)
Strafford. An Historical Tragedy (London: Longman, 1837)
Sordello (London: Edward Moxon, 1840)
Bells and Pomegranates I: Pippa Passes (London: Edward Moxon, 1841)
Bells and Pomegranates II: King Victor and King Charles (London: Edward Moxon, 1842)
Bells and Pomegranates III: Dramatic Lyrics (London: Edward Moxon, 1842)
Bells and Pomegranates IV: The Return of the Druses (London: Edward Moxon, 1843)
Bells and Pomegranates V: A Blot in the 'Scutcheon (London: Edward Moxon, 1843)
Bells and Pomegranates VI: Colombe's Birthday (London: Edward Moxon, 1844)
Bells and Pomegranates VII: Dramatic Romances and Lyrics (London: Edward Moxon, 1845)
Bells and Pomegranates VIII: "Luria" and "A Soul's Tragedy" (London: Edward Moxon, 1846)
Christmas-Eve and Easter Day (London: Chapman and Hall, 1850)
Men and Women, 2 vols. (London: Chapman and Hall, 1855)
Dramatis Personae (London: Chapman and Hall, 1864)
The Ring and the Book, 4 vols. (London: Smith and Elder, 1868–1869)
Balaustion's Adventure: Including a Transcript from Euripides (London: Smith and Elder, 1871)
Prince Hohenstiel-Schwangau, Saviour of Society (London: Smith and Elder, 1871)
Fifine at the Fair (London: Smith and Elder, 1872)
Red Cotton Night-Cap Country or Turf and Towers (London: Smith and Elder, 1873)
Aristophanes' Apology: Including a Transcript from Euripides, Being the Last Adventure of Balaustion (London: Smith and Elder, 1875)
The Inn Album (London: Smith and Elder, 1875)
Pacchiarotto and How He Worked in Distemper, with Other Poems (London: Smith and Elder, 1876)
The Agamemnon of Aeschylus (London: Smith and Elder, 1877)
La Saisiaz; The Two Poets of Croisic (London: Smith and Elder, 1878)
Dramatic Idyls, First Series (London: Smith and Elder, 1879)

Dramatic Idyls, Second Series (London: Smith and Elder, 1880)

Jocoseria (London: Smith and Elder, 1883)

Ferishtah's Fancies (London: Smith and Elder, 1884)

Parleyings with Certain People of Importance in Their Day (London: Smith and Elder, 1887)

Poetical Works of Robert Browning, 16 vols. (London: Smith and Elder, 1889)

Asolando: Fancies and Facts (London: Smith and Elder, 1889)

Modern Collected Editions

Jack, Ian et al., eds. *The Poetical Works of Robert Browning* (Oxford: Oxford University Press, 1984–). Five volumes have so far appeared; textually very sound and detailed, but the most expensive of the modern editions.

King, Roma et al., eds. *The Complete Poems of Robert Browning* (Athens: Ohio University Press 1969–). Nine volumes have so far appeared. The later volumes of this edition are mostly fine, but the first two contain a variety of errors that make them not the ideal choice for students of the poet.

Pettigrew, John, and Thomas Collins, eds. *Robert Browning: The Poems*, 2 vols. (Harmondsworth, England: Penguin, 1981); Richard Altick, ed., *The Ring and the Book* (Harmondsworth, England: Penguin, 1981). The cheapest, most accessible complete modern edition of the poetry and therefore often used by students and cited by critics, although the annotation is sometimes erratic.

Wooldford, John, and Daniel Karlin, eds. *The Poems of Browning* (Harlow, England: Longman, 1991–   ). Two volumes have so far appeared: not cheap, but the thoroughness of the annotation makes this probably the best edition of the poet available to us.

Letters

As of 1996, Browning's letters are scattered between a dozen or so volumes, making it very hard adequately to study them. When the complete *Browning's Correspondence* is finally available (edited by Kelley and Hudson—see below), this situation will change, but with forty projected volumes the edition will be many years in the editing. Until that time students have to sort their way through the following:

Collins, Thomas, ed. *The Brownings to the Tennysons* (Waco, Tex.: Wedgstone Press, 1971).

Curle, Richard, ed. *Robert Browning and Julia Wedgwood; A Broken Friendship as Revealed in Their Letters* (London: John Murray and Jonathan Cape, 1937).

DeVane, Clyde, and Kenneth Knickerbocker, eds. *New Letters of Robert Browning* (New Haven, Conn.: Yale University Press 1950).

DeLaura, David J. "Ruskin and the Brownings: Twenty-Five Unpublished Letters," *Bulletin of the John Rylands Library*, 54 (1972): 314–56.

Hood, Thurman, ed. *Letters of Robert Browning* (New Haven, Conn.: Yale University Press 1933).

Kelley, Philip, and Ronald Hudson, eds. *The Brownings' Correspondence* (Winfield, Kans.: Wedgstone Press, 1984–   ). Eleven volumes have so far appeared, out of a projected number of about forty.

Kenyon, F. G., ed. *The Letters of Elizabeth Barrett Browning*, 2 vols. (London: Smith and Elder, 1898).

Kintner, Elvan, ed. *The Letters of Robert Browning and Elizabeth Barrett, 1845–46*, 2 vols. (Cambridge, Mass.: Harvard University Press, 1969)

McAleer, Edward, ed. *Dearest Isa: Robert Browning's Letters to Isa Blagden* (Austin: University of Texas Press, 1951).

———, ed. *Learned Lady: Letters from Robert Browning to Mrs Thomas Fitzgerald 1876–1889* (Cambridge, Mass.: Harvard University Press, 1966).

Meredith, Michael, ed. *More Than Friend: The Letters of Robert Browning to Katharine de Kay Bronson* (Waco, Tex.: Wedgstone Press, 1985).

Peterson, William, ed. *Browning's Trumpeter: The Correspondence of Robert Browning and Frederick J. Furnivall, 1872–1889* (Washington, D.C.: Decatur, 1979).

SECONDARY SOURCES

1. Bibliography, Catalog, Handbook, and Concordance

Broughton, Leslie, and B. F. Stelter. *A Concordance to the Poems of Robert Browning*, 2 vols. (New York: G. E. Stechert, 1924–1925; 4 vol. reprint (New York: Haskell House, 1982). A well-constructed concordance, although (necessarily) bulky.

DeVane, William C. *A Browning Handbook* (1933; 2nd ed., New York: Appleton-Century-Crofts, 1955). Despite its occasional errors, this remains a well-nigh indispensable aid to the student of Browning.

Drew, Philip. *An Annotated Critical Bibliography of Robert Browning* (London: Harvester, 1990). A Sensible and comprehensive bibliography.

Kelley, Philip, and Betty Coley. *The Browning Collections: A Reconstruction with Other Memorabilia* (Waco, Tex.: Armstrong Browning Library/Wedgstone Press, 1984). An astonishing and fascinating piece of scholarship, telling us more or less exactly what Browning had in his library and therefore what he read.

2. Secondary Criticism: Books and Parts of Books

Altick, Richard, and James Loucks. *Browning's Murder Mystery Story: A Reading of "The Ring and the Book"* (Chicago: Univ. of Chicago Press, 1971). Comprehensive and convincing study of Browning's masterwork.

Armstrong, Isobel. "Browning and the Poetry of Sexual Love," in Armstrong, ed., *Writers and their Background: Robert Browning* (London, 1974). Study of Browning's representation of women as sexual beings.

Armstrong, Isobel. "Browning and the 'Grotesque' Style," in Armstrong, ed., *The Major Victorian Poets: Reconsiderations* (London: Routledge and Kegan Paul, 1969). "Grotesque" is Bagehot's term for Browning's style, meant originally as a criticism. Armstrong looks at the way we can see it as a virtue.

————. *Victorian Poetry: Poetry, Poetics and Politics* (London: Routledge, 1993). This general study contains excellent chapters on Browning (particularly chapter 11, "Browning in the 1850s and After") that consider him in the context of modern critical theory.

Bloom, Harold. *The Ringers in The Tower: Studies in the Romantic Tradition* (Chicago: University of Chicago Press, 1971). Includes an influential reading of "Childe Roland."

Bristow, Joseph. *Robert Browning* (New York: Harvester, 1991). A fairly up-to-date introductory study of Browning, divided into themes; good, if sometimes a little hostile (Bristow doesn't much like Browning's representation of women, for instance).

Corson, Hiram. *An Introduction to the Study of Robert Browning* (3rd ed., Boston 1903). An early, rather elementary study.

DeVane, Clyde. *Browning's Parleyings: the Autobiography of a Mind* (New Haven: Yale University Press, 1927). Very thorough reading of the *Parleyings*, relating them to the concerns of Browning's life.

Drew, Philip. *The Poetry of Browning: A Critical Introduction* (London: Methuen, 1970). This is straightforward, clear, and mentions the main elements. As an introductory study, though, Bristow's book is better.

Faas, Ekbert. *Retreat into the Mind: Victorian Poetry and the Rise of Psychiatry* (Princeton: Princeton Univ. Press, 1988). Fascinating and wide ranging study of the dramatic monologue as a precursor to psychiatry.

Griffiths, Eric. *The Printed Voice of Victorian Poetry* (Oxford: Oxford University Press 1989). This has some interesting things to say about the dramatic monologue (pp. 59–96), as well as a useful analysis of Browning's love poetry ("The Poetry of Being Married").

Honan, Park. *Browning's Characters: A Study in Poetic Technique* (New Haven: Yale University Press, 1961). Classic study of the development of Browning's "character revealing" techniques. Sometimes a little structuralist, but full of insight and sensitive reading.

Irvine, William, and Park Honan. *The Book, the Ring and the Poet: A Biography of Robert Browning* (London: Bodley Head, 1974). Although ostensibly a biography, this book contains a great deal by way of sensitive critical readings of Browning's poetry.

Jones, Sir Henry. *Browning as a Philosphical and Religious Teacher* (New York: Macmillan, 1891). One of the earliest critical treatments.

Karlin, Daniel. *Browning's Hatreds* (Oxford: Oxford University Press, 1993). An accessibly written and illuminating study of the "other" side of the poet (Browning is still often seen as a love poet or a poet of married life). Karlin sees him as a "good hater" and traces the importance of hatred to his work.

King, Roma A. *The Bow and the Lyre: The Art of Robert Browning* (Ann Arbor: University of Michigan Press, 1957).

————. *The Focusing Artifice: The Poetry of Robert Browning* (Athens: Ohio University Press, 1968). Sometimes infuriating, sometimes illuminating, King (particularly in the second work) at least takes a refreshingly comprehensive overview of Browning's career instead of pretending along with the majority of critics that he effectively stopped writing after *The Ring and the Book*. According to King's unconventional judgment, the four key poems for an understanding of Browning's art are *Sordello*, *The Ring and the Book*, *Fifine at the Fair* and *Parleyings with Certain People*.

Langbaum, Robert. *The Poetry of Experience: The Dramatic Monologue in Modern Literary Tradition* (New York: Random House, 1957; 2nd ed., 1963). This has the status of a classic in the world of Browning studies. Langbaum looks at the dramatic monologue in terms of "Sympathy versus Judgment."

Litzinger, Boyd, and Donald Smalley, eds. *Browning: the Critical Heritage* (London: Routledge and Kegan Paul 1970). Invaluable collection of reviews and other contemporary responses to Browning's poetry.

Martin, Loy D. *Browning's Dramatic Monologues and the Post-Romantic Subject* (Baltimore, Md.: John Hopkins University Press, 1985). An intelligent Marxist study of Browning's dramatic monologues.

Maynard, J. *Browning's Youth* (Cambridge, Mass.: Harvard University Press, 1977). Very detailed biographical-critical study of Browning's childhood and early manhood.

Miller, J. Hillis. *The Disappearance of God: Five Nineteenth-Century Writers* (Cambridge, Md.: Harvard University Press, 1963). Includes a stimulating chapter on Browning, although Miller's curious habit of not giving accessible references for his quotations can make it a little difficult to use.

Orr, Sutherland. *Life and Letters of Robert Browning* (1891; new ed., London: George Bell, 1908). Early biography by one of Browning's personal friends; remains a useful quarry for material.

Pearsall, Robert. *Robert Browning* (Twayne, 1974). Introductory study.

Raymond, William O. *The Infinite Moment and Other Essays in Robert Browning* (Toronto: University of Toronto Press, 1950; 2nd ed., 1965). A collection of Raymond's essays, including two ("The Infinite Moment" and "Browning's Dark Mood: A Study of *Fifine at the Fair*") that are well worth looking at.

Ryals, Clyde de L. *Browning's Later Poetry, 1871–1889* (Ithaca, New York: Cornell University Press, 1975). Study of the post-*Ring and the Book* poetry.

————. *The Life of Robert Browning: A Critical Biography* (Oxford: Blackwell, 1993). Perhaps not as good a biography as Irvine and Honan, but more up-to-date in its critical readings of individual works and surprisingly comprehensive for a relatively short work.

Shaw, W. David. *The Dialectical Temper: The Rhetorical Art of Robert Browning* (Ithaca, New York: Cornell University Press). Stimulating study, concentrating on the dialogue between "subjective" and "objective" in Browning's development.

Sinfield, Alan. *The Dramatic Monologue* (1977). Brief and lucid examination of the mode; says one or two things about Browning, but more useful as a contextual study.

Slinn, E. Warwick. *Browning and the Fictions of Identity* (Totowa, N.J.: Barnes and Noble, 1982). Slinn takes off from Langbaum's "action in character" to redefine the dramatic monologue as expressions of identity re-creation and self-fictionalization.

————. *The Discourse of Self in Victorian Poetry* (London: Macmillan, 1991). Later Slinn in out-and-out deconstructionist mode, tracing the shift from the metaphor of consciousness as self (Hegel) to the metaphor of consciousness as text (Derrida).

St. George, E. A. W. *Browning and Conversation* (London: Macmillan, 1993). As much a study of what Victorians expected of the art of "conversation" as a study of Browning's poetry (particularly the post-*Ring and Book* poetry) as an interactive activity.

Sullivan, Mary Rose. *Browning's Voices in "The Ring and the Book": A Study of Method and Meaning* (Toronto: University of Toronto Press, 1969). A fairly straightforward run through the main critical approaches to *The Ring and the Book*.

Tucker, Herbert F. *Browning's Beginnings: The Art of Disclosure* (Minneapolis: University of Minnesota Press, 1980). Arguably the best modern critical study of Browning. Tucker's main insight is that Browning's poetry opens up meaning instead of closing it down, that his art "is an art of disclosure" (rather than an art of "enclosure"), "an art that resists its own finalities" (5).

Whitla, William. *The Central Truth: The Incarnation in Robert Browning's Poetry* (Toronto: University of Toronto Press, 1963). Study of Browning's religious poetry, somewhat limited in looking only at representations of the incarnation.

Woolford, John. *Browning the Revisionary* (London: Macmillan, 1988). The title summarizes Woolford's argument that Browning deliberately revised and re-envisioned his own poetic project with each succeeding public failure, thereby forging his own particular literature.

3. Secondary Criticism: Articles

Culler, A. D. "Monodrama and the Dramatic Monologue," *PMLA* 90 (1975), 366–85. Suggestive article on different Victorian conceptions of interior monologue.

DeLaura, David J. "The Context of Browning's Painter Poems: Aesthetics, Polemics, Historics," *PMLA* 95 (1980), 367–88. Excellent article that locates Browning's aesthetics in contemporary debate.

Jerman, B. "Browning's Witless Duke," *PMLA* 72 (1957), 488–93. Reading of "My Last Duchess" as a study in unknowing self-revelation.

Karlin, Daniel. "Browning, Elizabeth Barrett, and 'Mesmerism,'" *Victorian Poetry* 27 (1989), 65–77. Intriguing look at a subject over which Browning and Elizabeth disagreed.

Perrine, Laurence. "Browning's Shrewd Duke," *PMLA* 74 (1959), 157–59. Direct response to Jerman's "Witless Duke" article.

Potkay, Adam. "The Problems of Identity and the Grounds for Judgement in *The Ring and the Book*," *Victorian Poetry* 25 (1987), 143–57. Potkay draws out the parallels between the narrator of book one (identified to a certain degree with Browning himself) and Guido.

Roberts, Adam. "Using Myth: Browning's *Fifine at the Fair*," *Browning Society Notes* 20 (1990), 12–30.

————. "Euripidaristophanizing: Browning's *Aristophanes' Apology*," *Browning Society Notes*, 21 (1991), 32–45. Examines the use of classical allusion as a smokescreen in *Aristophanes' Apology*.

Shaw, W. David. "Browning's Murder Mystery: *The Ring and the Book* and Modern Theory," *Victorian Poetry* 27 (1989), 79–98. Deconstructionist look at *The Ring and the Book*.

Siegchrist, Mark. "Type Needs Antitype: the Structure of Browning's *Parleyings*," *Victorian Newsletter*, 50 (1976), 1–10. An attempt to see overall structural unity in the *Parleyings*.

Tucker, Herbert F. "Epiphany and Browning: Character Made Manifest," *PMLA* 107 (October 1992), 1208–1221. Interesting article on the implications for "character" of Browning's monologues.

Index

The Author

Adam Roberts graduated from the universities of Aberdeen and Cambridge, and is currently Lecturer in English at Royal Holloway, University of London. He has published in scholarly journals on a variety of nineteenth-century topics, including Browning, Tennyson, Swinburne, and Dickens. He is currently editing an edition of Browning's poetry for the Oxford Authors series, and is an associate editor of *The Oxford Companion to Dickens*.